BIRD LIFE

A GUIDE TO THE BEHAVIOR AND BIOLOGY OF BIRDS

by
STEPHEN W. KRESS, Ph.D.
Research Biologist, National Audubon Society

Illustrated by
JOHN D. DAWSON

GOLDEN PRESS • NEW YORK
Western Publishing Company, Inc.
Racine, Wisconsin

FOREWORD

Birds surround us with their vibrant colors and songs. Even the most abundant species reward observers with opportunities to watch seldom-seen behaviors. This book is dedicated to those interested in going beyond identification of birds. It introduces such topics as bird behavior, family life, flight, migration, populations, and conservation. This final section—conservation—is a subject of great urgency.

Because birds require large amounts of clean food and air to maintain their high-speed lifestyles, they are sensitive indicators of the quality of their environments. When bird populations decline, human welfare is equally threatened. Yet protecting birds is more than prudent conservation for our own well-being. Bird conservation is an ethical responsibility that we must assume as stewards of the earth. We hold the future of the earth's 8,700 species of birds in our hands today. Each species is an irreplaceable treasure that must be carefully passed from our generation to that of our children.

S.W.K.

CONTENTS

THE NATURE OF BIRD BEHAVIOR

Birds and humans share many behaviors. Birds sing, court, defend their homes, and feed their young. Like some humans, most birds fly south in autumn to balmier climates. It's easy to identify with birds and to consider their behaviors in terms of our own. But most birds' senses of sight, hearing, orientation, and coordination far exceed those of humans.

Environments shape birds to look and behave in ways that help them survive in their varied habitats. Living birds have received from their ancestors many of their instinctive behaviors. Yet not all behavior is inherited. The behavior of birds is a mixture of instinctive skills and skills learned through experience.

Begging and feeding are instinctive behaviors.

American Robin

Northern Cardinal

Reflections often elicit instinctive territorial defense.

INSTINCTIVE behaviors, such as finding mates, locating food, avoiding predators, and rearing young, permit quick responses. While humans generally ponder a new situation before acting, birds usually act in a predictable manner whenever they see or hear a given stimulus, such as a mate or a predator. These instinctive behaviors are a quick way to respond to familiar situations. For example, when a male cardinal sees another male in his nesting territory, he usually chases it away. But sometimes the cardinal sees his own reflection in a window and attempts to chase it! This inappropriate response demonstrates that some birds cannot easily reason their way in new circumstances.

LEARNING is the ability to acquire new information. Birds that eat a wide variety of foods are usually the quickest to take advantage of new food sources and consequently must be considered the most intelligent. For example, such birds as gulls, crows, and ravens have diverse diets. They use varied feeding habits and have generalized beaks. These birds are usually quicker to learn than are those with specialized beaks and feeding habits, such as woodpeckers and flycatchers.

HABITUATION is a way of learning about new situations through repeated exposure. A plastic snake placed in a raspberry patch, for example, might scare the birds at first, but repeated exposure to it, without associated harm, will eventually teach the birds that this is a harmless situation. If the position of the snake is changed, the birds might have to rehabituate to the "snake."

Most birds habituate to human presence as long as they feel safe. For example, pigeons and sparrows in city parks are accustomed to the presence of humans. Even such wary birds as gulls and crows will lose their fear of humans if they are not harrassed.

PLAY is a form of learning since it helps coordinate motor and sensory skills. Young owls, for example, practice their pouncing behavior by jumping on such inanimate objects as seeds and pebbles. Like kittens and puppies, their play activity helps them improve their hunting skills with trial-and-error games. Some adult birds also play. Gulls, terns, ravens, crows, and eagles, as examples, sometimes drop sticks while in flight and then catch them before they hit the ground. Adult ravens sometimes slide down snowbanks feet first, riding on their tails!

Opportunistic feeders like these starlings learn quickly.

Young screech-owl practices hunting skill by pouncing on seeds—learning while "playing."

7

BODY CARE

All birds have feathers, and this common feature requires that they spend much of their time maintaining their plumage. Birds have surprisingly similar ways of bathing, oiling, and preening their feathers.

PREENING is the behavior in which a bird slides its beak over individual feathers in such a way that it connects the individual barbules (hooks) of the feather vanes together. Small birds, such as sparrows, may have 2,000 feathers, while larger birds, such as swans, may have as many as 25,000 feathers. Most feathers have a central shaft (rachis) and a wide region on either side called a vane. Preening restores separated barbules in the feather vane and helps the bird to maintain the feather surface.

Uropygial gland produces oil that birds spread on their feathers.

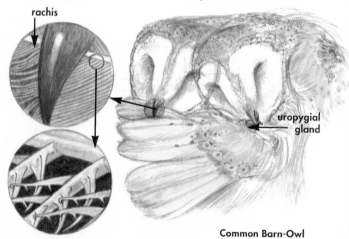

rachis

uropygial gland

Common Barn-Owl

detail of barbules

Mallard
female

Well-lubricated feathers shed water easily.

OILING is the feather-maintenance behavior in which birds squeeze their uropygial (oil) gland to lubricate their feathers. This nipplelike gland is located on the rump, just above the base of the tail. By squeezing and rubbing the beak sideways over the gland, a bird can use its beak to obtain oil and spread it onto the feathers while preening. This oil lubricates the tiny feather barbules and extends their life by helping to keep them from becoming too brittle. Well-lubricated and preened feathers also help to shed water and give the birds a waterproofed plumage. Water sheds off a duck's back (and even a sparrow's back) mainly because the feather barbules are so neatly connected that water does not have a chance to soak into the plumage. In some species the oil contains ergosterol, which converts into vitamin D when exposed to sunlight. When swallowed, the vitamin D helps prevent such diseases as rickets.

BATHING in water helps to clean the plumage. Some seabirds, such as terns, bathe on the surface of the ocean; others, like gulls, often fly to freshwater ponds and lakes for bathing. Robins and grackles bathe in roadside puddles, and hummingbirds sometimes bathe in the water that collects on large leaves. Where standing water is not available, cold-climate birds may bathe in snow, while hawks and vultures just spread their wings in the rain.

Regardless of a bird's size, the bathing behavior is similar. Birds typically first submerge their head, then quickly raise it and beat their wings in the water. This is usually followed by vigorous shaking, feather fluffing, preening, and oiling. Birdbaths are an excellent way to attract birds into your yard. Many species that do not readily come to feeders, such as catbirds and even screech-owls, will use birdbaths.

Birds use baths throughout the year to clean their feathers.

Eastern Screech-Owl

House Sparrows

Dust bathing helps eliminate feather parasites.

DUSTING is most common among birds that live in dry, open habitats, such as the Horned Lark, Ring-necked Pheasant, and some of the hawks and owls. House Sparrows, Ruffed Grouse, Wild Turkeys, wrens, kinglets, and quail also frequently dust bathe. House Sparrows seem to enjoy company as they dust bathe. Sometimes a dozen or more will gather, each scooping out a body-sized patch of dust in which it vigorously flutters its wings and spreads its tail while pressing its breast deep into the dust. While lying in the dust, they frequently peck and scratch with their feet. After dusting, the birds typically give their plumage several vigorous shakes to remove excess dust and then scratch their head and preen their feathers. Dusting probably helps to eliminate such parasites as feather lice and mites. Dusting may also function to remove excess oil, dandruff, and moisture that might otherwise cause feather matting. Most birds that bathe in dust usually do not take water baths.

11

SUNBATHING is known for at least 170 kinds of birds. Sunbathers typically face the sun while lying on a warm surface, such as a bare patch of soil or sidewalk. In typical sunning posture, the bird leans sideways, exposing one wing and half of its tail to direct sunshine. Sunning is a quick way to warm up, but there may be other reasons why so many birds expose themselves to full sunlight. Direct sunlight causes skin and feather parasites to concentrate under the wings or to climb to the top of the bird's head, where they are then dislodged by scratching and preening. Direct solar energy may also reduce a bird's need for food, since some of the sunlight provides useful energy through heat absorption. It is also believed that the warming of the oil produced by the preening gland stimulates formation of vitamins.

ANTING is a peculiar behavior in which birds spread their wings and tail while sitting atop an anthill or mound. This disturbs the ants, which then swarm through the birds' feathers. Some birds even grab the biting ants in their beaks and press them up into or rub them onto their feathers! The reasons for this unusual behavior are unclear, but it's likely that the biting ants help to reduce the itching or pain from new feathers that are growing, and they may also repel infestations of feather lice and other ectoparasites.

Mild-mannered ants are seldom used for anting. Most birds prefer ants that excrete such repugnant fluids as formic acid. Some birds use other strong-smelling items such as raw onion, orange peel, wasps, beetles, coffee, moth balls, cigarette butts, and even burning matches as ant substitutes. Over 200 bird species from around the world are known to "ant." These birds have used at least 24 different kinds of ants and over 40 substitute materials.

Sunning is a quick way to warm up.

American Robin

Northern Oriole

active anting

American Crow

passive anting

"Anting" may help birds reduce the number of skin parasites.

BILL WIPING is a common behavior in which birds wipe their beaks across a nearby perch or rough surface to remove excess food. The behavior usually follows feeding, but it is such a common behavior that it often surfaces at unusual times as a displacement behavior, an irrelevant and out-of-context act that occurs during stressful situations. Birds surprised by an intruder at their nest, for example, face the dilemma of either fleeing the nest site or defending it from the intruder. This conflict often results in the bird performing a displaced behavior that makes no sense at the time. Northern Ravens, for example, will sometimes uproot chunks of grass and fling them over their shoulder instead of chasing an intruder from their nests. When they are under stress, displacement behaviors in other birds may take the form of bathing, preening, nest-building, drinking, or singing.

Sometimes bill wiping functions as a displacement behavior.

Cedar
Waxwing

young Great Blue Heron

Panting permits heat to escape from a bird's moist mouth lining.

PANTING is one way birds can cool off. Unlike humans and most mammals, birds do not have sweat glands and cannot perspire to help cool themselves. Instead they expose their mouth lining to the air to release excess heat. Heat transfer from the mouth lining is a very effective way of releasing excess heat. In very hot situations, birds will further decrease their body temperature by fluttering their throat. This is an especially important behavior for baby birds whose nests may be located in the tops of trees or in exposed places on the ground where they cannot retreat to a cooler place.

The mechanism for controlling panting in birds is located in the midbrain. If the brain temperature in a pigeon increases by 2 degrees (from 107 to 109 degrees F), its breathing rate will make a dramatic increase from 46 to 150 times per minute. At this higher temperature, it passes three times as much air over its mouth lining and through its lungs and air sacs.

15

Sleeping Mallard tucks head under shoulder feathers.

Bluebirds conserve body heat by huddling.

SLEEPING birds are seldom seen because they usually find out-of-the-way places to rest. Most land birds sleep in the same habitat in which they nest, but they usually do not sleep on the nest unless they are incubating eggs. Most woodpeckers, for example, excavate separate sleeping cavities in which they spend the night, but some individuals prefer to sleep in abandoned cup-shaped nests of robins and other birds. Catbirds, robins, doves, and jays usually roost in dense shrubs and bushes.

Brown Creepers sleep by themselves, tucked into tree bark, while blackbirds and starlings prefer to sleep with others of their kind in large groups called roosts. Their winter roosts often contain a million birds, and some have been estimated to contain as many as 15 million. Sleeping in large roosts offers protection from such nocturnal predators as owls.

Shorebirds, such as sandpipers, pelicans, ducks, geese, and gulls, usually sleep on land at remote sites—for

16

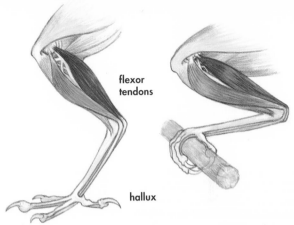

flexor
tendons

hallux

Flexor tendons help lock perching birds' feet on branches for sleeping.

instance, on islands or points of land. They are safer there from predatory mammals. Most water birds, such as gulls, terns, and ducks, sleep at night while floating at sea or on a pond, lake, or river. Ruffed Grouse may sleep in a snowbank, while the European Swift sometimes sleeps in flight. Birds that roost on the ground, such as the Northern Bobwhite, usually roost in a tight circle and press their bodies close together to share body heat. Cavity-nesting birds, such as chickadees and bluebirds, also huddle together in tree cavities and nest boxes.

Most birds have a characteristic sleeping posture in which they lay their head on their back and tuck their beak into their shoulder feathers. Birds that perch on open branches lock themselves in place while they sleep. As the bird squats on its tree-limb roost while sleeping, the flexor tendons automatically tighten the toes around the perch. When the bird stands up, the flexor tendons relax, and the bird's foot opens.

FEEDING BEHAVIORS

The beaks of most birds are specialized for eating a particular kind of food, but careful observation shows most eat a great variety. Competition between species is avoided by feeding at different times of the day or night, at different places on trees, at different water depths, or even by probing at different depths into mud.

HAWKING is a method of catching flying insects. Typically, a bird perches atop a tall tree or at the end of a dead branch. It flies out, captures a flying insect, and then returns to the same perch to wait for another. Cedar Waxwings and such flycatchers as kingbirds and Olive-sided Flycatchers capture large insects such as dragonflies that come within range. Flycatchers have large, flattened beaks with which they snatch and grip their prey. Sensitive bristles at the edges of their beak may help them determine when to open it, and a sharp hook on the tip permits them to keep a tight grip.

Kingbirds capture their prey by hawking.

One type of gleaning: perched Black-throated Green Warbler plucks insects and spiders from branches and twigs.

GLEANING is a type of insect-capturing behavior in which the bird picks insects off leaves, stems, tree trunks, and other surfaces. Most small insect-eating birds, such as warblers, chickadees, and titmice, glean while they remain perched. Red-eyed Vireos and such small flycatchers as the Least, Acadian, and Willow scan vegetation, then fly out and grab their prey. Kinglets, Great Crested Flycatchers, and phoebes pick insects off branches or walls while hovering. These variations permit closely related birds to find foods in the same habitats.

19

Black-and-white
Warbler

American Woodcock

White-breasted Nuthatch

Brown Creeper

Woodcock probes deep in soil. Some birds probe
cracks in tree bark.

PROBING is a feeding behavior in which birds reach into
tree bark, mud, or soil in search of insects and worms.
Shorebirds, such as sandpipers, dowitchers, and
Common Snipes, get most of their food by probing into
mud with their beak for worms and tiny crustaceans. Each
kind of shorebird has either a different length beak or a
different manner or depth of probing.

Three master probers are American Woodcocks,
Common Snipes, and dowitchers, but they live in different
habitats and thus avoid competition. Woodcocks frequent
overgrown, upland fields. The Common Snipe lives in wet,
swampy fields. Dowitchers inhabit open mudflats. All
probe deep into the soil and mud, and they can spread the
flexible tip of their beak to capture worms and other prey
underground. Nuthatches, Brown Creepers, and Black-
and-white Warblers probe cracks and crevices in tree bark.
They avoid competing by probing from different angles
and at different locations on tree trunks and branches.

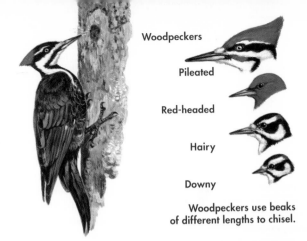

Woodpeckers

Pileated

Red-headed

Hairy

Downy

**Woodpeckers use beaks
of different lengths to chisel.**

CHISELING is the usual feeding behavior of woodpeckers. Their stout, sturdy beak is well adapted for whacking at wood. Most woodpeckers use their beak to open holes through the bark to gain access to boring insects. Hairlike bristles protect their nostrils from flying sawdust and wood chips. A cushioned skull prevents headaches.

Like the shorebirds that have various length beaks for probing at different depths into mud, woodpeckers have different length beaks that permit access to insects inhabiting various levels in the bark and tree interiors. They also have a very long, coiled tongue. Downy Woodpeckers, for example, have the shortest beaks and make the shallowest intrusions. Their short beak allows them to feed on very small twigs and even weed stalks that are too small for larger woodpeckers. In contrast, the crow-sized Pileated Woodpecker can chisel many inches into trees and can fling wood chips 3 inches long. Woodpeckers depend on their hearing to detect the gnawing sounds of carpenter ants and wood-boring beetle larvae and the buzzing wings of overwintering cluster flies.

LEAF-TOSSING is a common feeding behavior of such ground-feeding birds as towhees, thrashers, White-throated Sparrows, Fox Sparrows, and Ruffed Grouse. By scratching at loose leaves, these birds expose beetles, caterpillars, ants, and other hidden insects.

In a behavior called foot-raking, many kinds of herons, egrets, cranes, and storks use their feet to disturb the muddy bottom in order to spook crayfish, tadpoles, small fish, and other animals into striking range. Wood Storks stir the bottom with their pink toes and then swing their open beak through the muddy water to feel for moving fish. Likewise, Snowy Egrets stir the bottom with their bright yellow feet, which may help to spook small fish into striking range. Foot-stamping is a similar foot action used on muddy soil by Herring Gulls and some cranes. Their stamping creates rapid vibrations that cause earthworms to come to the surface where they become easy prey.

Birds may use their feet to kick aside leaves
or other debris or to make a commotion
that stirs small animals into moving.

Rufous-sided Towhee

Common Nighthawk

rictal bristles

Birds that sweep for their insect prey usually have sensitive rictal bristles and a large mouth.

SWEEPING is a feeding technique in which a fast-flying bird, such as a swallow, nighthawk, or swift, opens its beak, captures its prey, and then swallows the prey in mid-flight. These birds do not fly about looking for food with their mouth wide open. They locate their prey by sight, then swoop in and open their beak just in time to snap up the flying insect. Birds that feed in this manner have very large mouths and surprisingly small beaks. Most also have a set of modified rictal bristles that look more like eyelashes than feathers. These create a sensitive "insect net" around the mouth. When an insect touches the bristles, the bird quickly snaps it up.

23

DIVING birds, such as loons, grebes, puffins, and certain ducks, have many unique adaptations. They are, for example, heavier than surface-swimming water birds of the same size. They have solid bones and more massive bodies. Without this extra weight, diving birds would be too buoyant to dive to great depths. Some penguins even swallow stones, presumably as ballast to achieve extra weight and easier control under the water. Cylinder-shaped bodies enhance streamlining, and propellerlike legs positioned far to the rear help them in powerful dives. Some birds even extend their wings and "fly" underwater. Large amounts of fat and dense down insulate them from frigid water.

Some divers reach remarkable depths. Atlantic Puffins may dive to 200 feet. The Emperor Penguin, the largest diving bird, may dive to 875 feet. Most diving birds stay under for less than a minute, but Emperor Penguins can stay under for up to 18 minutes.

Closely related species dive to different depths, presumably to avoid competition for food.

Black Guillemot

165 ft.
200 ft.

400 ft.

Razorbill

Atlantic Puffin

600 ft.

Common Murre

Plunge-diving is another way of breaking through the water surface. Buoyant birds, such as kingfishers, Brown Pelicans, gannets, and boobies, plunge into the sea from heights as great as 100 feet.

STOOPING is a high-speed aerial pursuit performed by certain hawks, especially large falcons. The Peregrine Falcon is the most accomplished. It can see small birds at least 3,000 feet away as it hunts by flying over open habitat. Peregrines start their stoop by pumping their wings to build up speed, then pull their wings partway to their sides and plunge downward. Building up speeds of at least 175 mph, they usually snatch small prey, such as finches, from the air with their long, sharp talons. They stun larger birds by punching them, using their feet like a closed fist, then follow their prey to the ground.

Peregrine Falcons can reach speeds of 175 mph while stooping.

DABBLING is a common feeding behavior for surface-feeding ducks, geese, and swans. In contrast to their diving-duck relatives, dabbling ducks are very buoyant and usually feed in shallow water where they typically turn upside down—their legs kicking at the surface and their tail pointed straight up while they reach to the bottom of the marsh or pond edge in search of submerged plants, small fish, tadpoles, and such invertebrates as insects, snails, and worms that hide in the mud. Because their feet are located toward the rear of their body, diving ducks must run across the water to take wing, while dabbling ducks can leap directly into the air.

Geese sometimes dabble but usually graze on land, feeding on plant sprouts, spilled grain, and such invertebrates as earthworms and beetle larvae. In contrast, swans use their long necks to stretch to the pond bottom in search of food that is generally beyond the reach of dabbling ducks. In this way, competition is avoided.

Waterfowl avoid competing by feeding in different habitats and on different foods.

Canada Goose

Tundra Swan

Mallard

Green-backed Herons sometimes use bread as bait.

STALKING birds walk slowly along the ground or wade through shallow water searching for their prey. American Robins appear to be listening for their quarry, but they are actually turning their head to get a better view as they watch for slight movements that give away the location of the worms. Then, with a sudden jab, they grab and pull the worm to the surface. Herons and plovers stalk for food in different habitats but feed in a similar way. Herons walk slowly through the shallow water looking down for movement of an unwary fish or frog, or they may stand and wait. In a similar way, plovers patrol beaches, just as robins stalk a lawn, always alert for the slightest movement. Green-backed Herons have a novel way of luring small fish within striking range. When bread or similar bait is available, they sometimes drop a piece on the surface and wait until fish come up for it.

Bald Eagles sometimes chase Ospreys, attempting to steal fish.

PIRACY occurs when one bird steals food from another. Successful pirates are usually larger than the birds from which they steal. For example, Bald Eagles sometimes chase Ospreys and make them drop their prey. If the pirate is successful, it picks up the food (often intercepting it in midair) and either eats it or carries it back to its nest. Piracy is most common during the nesting season when food demands are greatest. Herring Gulls try to steal food from puffins if they get a chance, but puffins dash to their nest with fish and usually make a delivery without interference. Frigatebirds were even named for their habit of taking food on the wing. Like the infamous frigate ships, frigatebirds wait for an unsuspecting victim to return to its nest carrying food, then swoop after the meal with remarkable grace. They can sometimes tell if another bird is carrying food by listening to the sounds it makes!

SCAVENGING is the consumption of dead animals. Gulls, crows, ravens, and vultures are the most common scavengers. They clean up animals killed along highways and those that die in the field or along beaches. Likewise, Bald Eagles often feed on fish carrion found along lakes and rivers—especially in the winter when waterways are frozen and fishing for live food is difficult. Most scavengers locate their prey by keen eyesight, but Turkey Vultures can find food with their unusually good sense of smell. They are so dependent on locating food by smell that they sometimes ignore carrion unless it gives off an appropriate odor. In contrast, Black Vultures use their keen eyesight for locating carrion. In this way, the two species find different food and thus avoid competition.

Scavengers clean up roadside kills quickly.

American Crows

COOPERATIVE FEEDING

Sometimes many individuals of the same or different species group together in a joint feeding effort. Many seabirds, such as terns and gannets, feed in loose groups over schools of fish that may be chased to the surface by even larger fish. Flashing wings and plunge-diving apparently help to signal that food is at hand.

Feeding flocks of mixed species commonly occur when schools of fish are discovered; sometimes these groups work together and are thus more successful when fishing.

Anhingas, cormorants, and pelicans may improve their feeding efficiency by forming bands to drive schools of fish into shallow water where they are more easily captured.

White Pelicans herd fish into shallows where they are easily caught.

Cattle Egrets usually feed with cattle.

Sometimes these flocks show organized, coordinated behavior. Groups of White Pelicans may form an arc or semicircular pattern and swim toward shore, thrashing their wings and herding small fish in front of them. In a similar way, American Avocets and Black-necked Stilts sometimes form impressive wedge-shaped formations containing hundreds of birds that beat the water with their long, thin beaks. This beating stirs fish and insects to the surface and acts to confuse the prey while increasing the chances of an individual bird obtaining a meal.

Many birds also benefit by feeding near other animals that serve as "beaters" for them. One study found that Cattle Egrets feeding behind cattle capture 3.6 times more insects than do those that feed by themselves. Other birds, such as gulls and crows, have learned that worms and grubs stirred up by tractors become easy meals. Such benefits often lead to cooperative feeding.

FOOD STORAGE

Resident (nonmigratory) birds that winter in harsh habitats often store (cache) food. Food storing is vital for many cold-climate birds, such as titmice, chickadees, nutcrackers, and jays. In late summer and fall, many nonmigratory birds start hiding insects, grains, acorns, and other foods in tree crevices, cracks in bark, and holes in the ground.

The energy devoted to storing food is often astounding. For example, Acorn Woodpeckers dig a snug hole for each stored acorn and may sometimes stash as many as 50,000 acorns in one tree! Even some predatory birds such as the Northern Hawk-Owl and the Great Gray Owl will sometimes cache mice or other food in hollow trees. Shrikes store food on thorns or barbed wire.

Birds that build up winter food caches are usually

Acorn Woodpeckers sometimes store thousands of acorns.

Northern Shrikes can remember where they stored prey up to eight months later.

capable of digging up their buried treasure even when it is hidden by several inches of snow. One study found that Clark's Nutcrackers will dig 8 inches through the snow to uncover seed cones that were buried months earlier. Likewise, shrikes can remember where they left their prey up to eight months later. Some birds, such as Clark's Nutcracker, show altruistic behavior by contributing pine seeds and hazel nuts to a communal cache near their nesting area. The following spring, members of the flock all draw on this food supply.

Some birds start storing for the lean winter months during the fall when food is plentiful, but the food-storing behavior in some species, such as ravens, is triggered by hunger. Hungry ravens are more likely to cache food than are those that are well fed. Since even very young ravens store food, it is likely that the caching behavior is instinctive.

SOCIAL DISPLAYS

Even before a bird leaves its egg, it communicates with appropriate behaviors. Some hatching chicks cause their parents to switch from incubating to brooding behavior by making sounds, signaling that they will soon hatch. After hatching, nestlings exhibit the proper behaviors in order to be fed and brooded. Later, appropriate social behaviors are necessary when finding a mate.

Flocking species, such as blackbirds, waxwings, and finches, must also interact with flock members. While such behaviors as soliciting food from parents are clearly instinctive, some species may learn mate selection and migration skills. Birds communicate with each other through a complex series of visual and sound displays that collectively represent their social behavior.

ROOSTS are places where birds sleep. Many birds come together at night because there is safety in numbers from predators and for the added advantage of shared body heat. The proximity birds tolerate with each other depends in large part on air temperature. On the coldest winter nights, ten or more Eastern Bluebirds will huddle together inside tree cavities and nest boxes. Likewise, on cold nights, Inca Doves in the southwestern United States are known to sleep in a feathery mass several layers deep. In a similar response, Common Bushtits usually perch on branches no closer than 2 inches apart, but on unusually cool winter nights, they huddle shoulder to shoulder. Such social huddling may have other advantages, however, since many tropical species, such as Prong-billed Barbets and wood-swallows, also huddle together on tree branches even though they live in habitats that are far from frigid.

Mallards sleep in large rafts on open water.

Some birds that live solitary lives by day roost in large numbers at night.

Chimney Swifts

FORAGING FLOCKS of land birds are common, especially during winter. Mixed flocks containing several chickadees, titmice, woodpeckers, and nuthatches are a common sight in North American forests. Mixed-species flocks containing both nonmigrants and migrants also occur in the tropics, where several dozen birds of a dozen or more species may move through the forest together. Such flocking helps birds avoid predatory hawks, for many more eyes are watching.

Birds can also find more food by feeding in flocks, as they can spend more time searching for food and less time watching for predators. Each species in the mixed flock feeds on a somewhat different food, and so there is usually little competition. Some ornithologists theorize that blackbirds, herons, and many colonial water birds may share information about food supplies. For example, blackbirds, which are the first to leave their roost in the morning, may be followed by those looking for a new feeding place.

Many birds look for food in mixed foraging flocks.

dominant posture

Black-capped Chickadees

submissive posture

Dominant chickadee usually opens its beak, holds its head forward, and partly spreads its tail and wings.

PECK ORDERS give social rank to birds by identifying which birds are dominant. This social hierarchy is most conspicuous among such birds as chickens, crows, and shorebirds that spend most of their time in flocks. Peck orders also exist among family members.

Sex and age, for example, are the dominant characteristics that define dominance in chickadees and titmice. Chickadees form small winter flocks of six to ten birds, with one pair dominant. Often there are short chases between members of the group, since the dominant pair establishes a hierarchy in which both the male and the female become dominant over other flock members of their sex. Dominance brings with it the benefits of priority feeding and watering opportunities and the warmest spot in the night roost. Most peck orders are established through displays in which the dominant bird leans forward with its beak open while its wings and tail are partially spread.

Crows chase Great Horned Owls from their territories.

MOBBING is a group effort in which birds chase a predator. When a predator such as an owl, fox, or human approaches too close to an active bird nest, the intruder may be greeted by alarm calls and chased by many nesting birds. Owls are frequent targets for mobbing. Most land birds are relatively defenseless at dusk and during the night, but birds that chase owls from their territories during daylight are less likely to suffer predation from that owl after dark.

Terns are quick to take wing at the approach of a crow, raven, hawk, or other predator. To banish an intruder from their colony, dozens may mount an attack by diving, screaming, and squirting excrement. Most flying predators readily retreat from the sharp-beaked terns. Mobbing is such a fundamental instinct that birds can sometimes be fooled into attacking decoy owls and snakes. Most birds, however, soon recognize the difference between real threats and imitations.

Killdeer lures predator away from nest.

DISTRACTION DISPLAYS can lead predators away from the nests and young of ground-nesting birds. Birds varying in size from the Ostrich to the Black-and-white Warbler sometimes lure predators away from their nests and young by struggling on the ground with one wing outstretched and giving pitiful cries as if the wing were broken. Predators, including humans, cats, dogs, and even snakes, usually stalk the conspicuous adult only to find that the "crippled" bird quickly "recovers."

This distraction display at first seems to be a good example of an intelligent, purposeful action, but it probably results from a conflict of behaviors. Parent birds possibly feel two responses: an impulse to attack the predator to defend the nest or young, and a desire to flee. The parent is thrown into a frenzy. Many generations of natural selection have favored certain aspects of the performance.

FAMILY LIFE

All birds lay eggs, and most build nests. Within these constants, there is remarkable variation in the ways in which birds rear their young. At one extreme, Australian Brush Turkeys lay their eggs in a great mound of rotting vegetation, which warms the eggs. When the young hatch, they dig to the surface and start life completely independent of their parents. At the opposite extreme, frigatebirds carefully incubate their single egg for around 60 days and then feed their dependent youngster for more than a year after hatching.

TERRITORIES are defended areas used for feeding, sleeping, or the rearing of young. Animals ranging in size from elephants to tiny ants share the common need for such private places. In a world crowded with so many different kinds of animals, the need for ample private space goes a long way toward maintaining order. Since this powerful drive is one of the most widespread animal behaviors, it is not surprising that most birds establish and maintain territories in which they attempt to exclude others of their species.

Nesting territories help insure adequate food for the parents and young; protect the young from interference by other members of their species; provide familiarity with habitat and thus increase foraging efficiency; regulate populations by limiting the number of pairs that can be accommodated in a specific area; reduce losses from predation by scattering nests; identify a site to which parents can return in subsequent years, thus helping experienced birds to nest again in sites where they were previously successful; and, finally, reduce the chances of having matings "stolen" by intruding males.

Male Indigo Buntings defend their territory by singing. If song is ignored, they will chase an intruder away, past their territory's border.

41

SIZES OF NESTING TERRITORIES vary depending upon the quality of the nesting habitat. Each species has its own preference for the "ideal" combination of food, water, cover, and nest sites.

When birds find quality habitat, they usually set up relatively small territories. Less desirable habitat necessitates larger territories, which are more difficult to defend and require more effort by the resident birds. Ovenbirds, for example, prefer aspen forests in Ontario, where they usually have territories covering less than an acre. In contrast, Ovenbirds in mature maple forests usually defend territories that are larger than 4 acres. Larger territories may, however, offer a greater variety of foods and thus provide backup food supplies.

Territory size may also change over the course of the breeding season. One study in Utah found that when Black-capped Chickadees were building nests, the males

42

defended territories averaging 5.8 acres, but the birds used only .9 acres of the territory while they were incubating their eggs and rearing young. Once the young left the nest, the families used about 2 acres.

In large areas of uniform habitat, such as forests and grasslands, all suitable habitat is often occupied by adjacent territories that form a mosaic over the land. Likewise, dippers, kingfishers, the Louisiana Waterthrush, and other birds that nest along streams often defend linear territories that follow the stream and extend only a few feet up the banks. Colonial land birds, such as Purple Martins and Bank Swallows, typically defend only their nest site, since they often feed far from the colony. Colonial water birds, such as herons, terns, and gulls, also nest within a few feet of their nearest neighbors. Like swallows that feed far from the colony on patchy food supplies, these water birds often travel miles away from the nest to obtain food.

Song Sparrows in a salt marsh establish and defend their own individual territories.

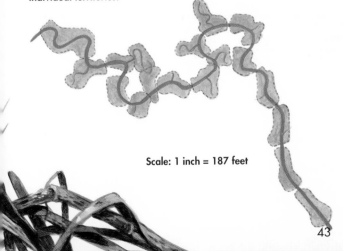

Scale: 1 inch = 187 feet

DEFENDING TERRITORIES While human territories (home and country) are generally defended by customs, physical barriers, laws, and police force, birds usually defend their territories with song and displays of bright feathers. They rarely resort to combat.

In spring, adult males of most migratory species typically return to their nesting habitat before females arrive. Red-winged Blackbirds and Song Sparrows are among the earliest arrivals. They start singing soon after returning to familiar haunts. The first males have their choice of habitats, and they select territories where they are most likely to attract a mate and rear young. Later arrivals must occupy marginal habitat that may not have as much food or cover or as many perches.

Early arrivals can select prime nesting habitat, but they run the risk of arriving before food is available. Woodcocks arriving too early, for example, cannot probe in the frozen soil for earthworms. Likewise, Purple Martins sometimes arrive in the north before there are ample flying insects to sustain them, and thousands die from hunger.

SONG PLAYS A CENTRAL ROLE in the defense of territories. When a male first claims his territory, he announces his intent to breed by singing from conspicuous perches. Some birds not only announce their territorial claims with song, but also flash brilliant colors. The Red-winged Blackbird, for example, produces a harsh "okareee" call, then displays his gaudy red shoulder patches. When he is not actively defending his territory, his red shoulders are typically hidden.

Birds on established territories usually have an advantage over intruding rivals. Even if the rival is larger, stronger, and more colorful, it is generally discouraged by the songs and chases of the resident male.

at rest

Male Red-winged Blackbirds flutter their wings and display flashy shoulder epaulettes to advertise their presence.

displaying epaulettes

45

COURTSHIP STATIONS are territories where males display in order to attract mates. Unlike nesting territories where males defend their space, mates, and nests and also find food for their young, males that defend courtship stations only use the site to attract and fertilize mates. Males with courtship stations chase intruding males away and perform elaborate rituals that advertise their presence. Birds such as woodcocks, prairie-chickens, and hummingbirds defend courtship stations rather than nesting territories.

American Woodcocks are a good example of a species that uses courtship stations. For their sunset dance, male woodcocks usually select a patch of very short grass surrounded by a brushy field. Each excited male parades on his courting territory. After producing several nasal "peents," he bursts into a spiraling flight in which he may climb to 300 feet, then drop like a falling leaf. This wild display attracts females and discourages other males from attempting to steal his courting station.

Allen's
Hummingbird

Male hummingbirds perform courtship flights at locations called courtship stations.

Hooded Warblers defend winter territories in the tropics.

WINTER TERRITORIES are the rule for many land birds that travel to the tropics during winter months. Long-distance migrants, such as the American Redstart, Hooded Warbler, and Northern Waterthrush, migrate from northern deciduous forests in the United States and winter in tropical forests of Central America. These species sing songs similar to those used on their nesting grounds and will actively defend their territories from intruding members of their species. Winter territories are about the same size as breeding territories and usually occur in similar habitats. While males and females share their breeding territory, each sex defends its own winter territory.

Some nonmigrants, such as the Red-headed Woodpecker and the Plain Titmouse, also defend winter territories. Carolina Wrens typically form permanent pair bonds, and both sexes defend the territory throughout the year. Females watch for predators; the male sings and patrols the borders for intruding Carolina Wrens.

MATING

To breed successfully, most birds first establish a territory and then proceed to attract a mate of the proper species, sex, and age. Time is of the essence for both male and female, since most birds live only a few years.

BREEDING AGE varies greatly from one species to the next, but in general it is related to life span. Song Sparrows, chickadees, finches, and most other backyard birds breed for the first time during the first spring following their hatching. They are only about 10 or 11 months old. Breeding at such an early age is important since these birds usually live only 2 to 3 years. In contrast, long-lived birds, such as puffins (which often live to 20 years) usually do not breed until they are 5 or 6 years old. The Royal Albatross may wait until it is 11 years old.

Males and females usually breed at the same age, but females sometimes breed a year earlier than do males. With Red-winged Blackbirds and Herring Gulls, for example, males must compete with each other to establish a nesting territory, and older birds often claim most of the suitable habitat. In contrast, young females are readily accepted into established territories.

SUNLIGHT PLAYS AN IMPORTANT ROLE in initiating the nesting cycle. As day length increases in late winter, the anterior pituitary gland produces hormones that trigger the gonads to produce sex hormones—androgens in males and estrogens in females.

Birds receive some light through their eyes, but they also detect sunlight and changes in day length through the skin on top of their head. The red wavelength provides the greatest stimulus to hormone production.

Male Red-winged Blackbirds usually nest for the first time when they are two years old, females when they are one year old.

male

immature male

female

Long-lived birds, such as the Royal Albatross, may not breed until they are 11 years old.

49

Male Common Tern offers small fish to prospective mate.

Male Roseate Spoonbill offers nesting material.

COURTSHIP RITUALS permit birds to pair with a mate of the same species that is at the same stage in the breeding cycle. When a male Common Tern is looking for a prospective mate, for example, he offers a small fish. If the female does not flutter her wings in a submissive posture and swallow the fish, the male loses interest.

Male herons, spoonbills, pelicans, and cormorants pass sticks or seaweed to prospective mates as a courtship ritual. If the female starts building a nest with the gift, the pair will probably proceed through the nesting cycle.

Food and nest-material offerings serve to demonstrate the ability of the male as a provider and may help the female to assess the male's skill at finding food, a quality that will prove vital once the young have hatched. Such gifts are reminders that in nearly all bird species, the female is the one that actually selects a mate, since she accepts or rejects the initial courtship gestures.

male

female

whisker mark

Male and female Northern Flickers look almost identical.

BIRDS CAN OFTEN RECOGNIZE THEIR MATES by subtle differences in the size and proportion of beak and head and by differences in vocalizations. Species in which the sexes have identical plumages, such as gannets, gulls, terns, and the Cedar Waxwing, are especially capable of recognizing such subtle characteristics.

A study using Northern Flickers showed the importance of these subtle plumage differences. Males and females look almost identical, but the male has a whisker mark on his face, while the female's face is unmarked. The importance of this mark for mate recognition became very apparent when researchers painted black whiskers onto a female and released her near her nest. When the male found this bewhiskered female back at their nest, he chased her away, presumably confusing her with an intruding male. He did not accept the female until the whisker marks were removed.

MONOGAMOUS PAIR BONDS are the usual mating arrangement for most birds. In this pair bond, one male pairs with a single female, and the two cooperate to raise young. This arrangement helps to insure that the eggs and young receive adequate care, food, and protection during the incubation and chick-rearing periods.

POLYGAMOUS PAIR BONDS, in which one male or one female mates with several members of the opposite sex, are the rule for birds nesting in food-rich habitat.

Males often form polygynous relationships in which each male mates with several females. While the male defends its territory from other male intruders, each female incubates her clutch and rears the young with little help from the male. Bobolinks, Red-winged Blackbirds, and Ring-necked Pheasants are polygynous.

More unusual are polyandrous relationships that occur when a female pairs with several males. A female Spotted Sandpiper, for example, lays eggs in several nests, and different males incubate each nest. Polyandrous females maximize production by reducing time spent incubating eggs and protecting young.

PROMISCUOUS MATINGS also occur in such food-rich habitats as meadows and marshes. In these relationships, males set up courting areas in which they attract females for mating. After mating, the females build a nest somewhere nearby, incubate the eggs, and raise the young. Woodcocks, hummingbirds, and prairie-chickens are examples of birds that mate promiscuously. Females that rear young following promiscuous matings either have very small broods, like the hummingbirds, or have precocial (well-developed) young that feed themselves, like the prairie-chickens.

Northern Cardinals, like most birds, have monogamous pair bonds.

Ring-necked Pheasants have polygynous relationships.

Ruby-throated Hummingbirds mate promiscuously.

male

female

53

NEST HELPERS occur among many species, including certain kingfishers, hawks, jays, tanagers, and wrens. Helpers are generally younger adults that assist their parents in rearing nestlings.

Some colonial birds, such as White-fronted Bee-eaters of eastern Africa, live in groups of 200 birds associated with only 30 to 60 nests. About half the pairs in the colony are assisted by helpers that are usually sons and daughters. Many solitary species, such as the Southern House Wren and the Australian Kookaburras, also have helpers at their nest.

Helpers generally do all of the usual nest-associated behaviors, such as building nests, incubating eggs, guarding nestlings, cleaning the nest, and feeding young. With such help, it's not surprising that several studies have shown that pairs with nest helpers can rear more young than those without helpers. Kookaburras without helpers, for example, raised an average of 1.2 young per nest; pairs with helpers raised 2.3 young per nest.

Helping behavior seems to be altruistic in that it is of no obvious benefit to the helper, but recent studies with bee-eaters have shown that fathers often break up the nests of their one- and two-year-old sons, forcing the offspring to abandon their own nest and help the parents raise another brood. Long-term studies have generally shown that most helpers are waiting for an opportunity to breed and that once they get a chance to nest, they soon set up territories and start rearing their own young.

While most helpers assist their parents, there are also many examples of adults feeding young of different species. Parent Barn Swallows may, for example, feed fledgling Cliff Swallows. Robins have been known to feed young grackles. Northern Cardinals that have lost young have even fed gulping goldfish in a backyard pool!

Young White-fronted Bee-eaters (above) and Florida Scrub Jays (below) help parents rear the next generation.

55

BUILDING A NEST

The location, size, and dimensions of a nest reflect the size of the family and such factors as weather extremes, threats from predators, and availability of nesting materials. The nest is the focus of family life.

LOCATION has a great influence on the size and shape of the nest. Beach-nesting birds, such as the Piping Plover and the Least Tern, hide their speckled eggs by simply making a scrape in bare sand. The females of most ground-nesting birds, such as Bobolinks, ducks, grouse, meadowlarks, and sparrows, have well-camouflaged, striped backs, a pattern that helps hide the location of the nest. These parents typically sit so tight while incubating that a predator may pass within inches of the nest before the parent flushes. When threatened by predators, ground-nesting birds may dive aggressively or lure the predator away with distraction displays (p. 39).

Many birds are very picky when selecting nest sites. Cactus Wrens, for example, orient their nest in one direction in spring to avoid cold winds, in another direction in summer to expose the nest to cooling breezes.

Many species put their nests in locations that offer protection from predators. Northern Mockingbirds, for example, usually nest in thorny shrubs, while birds ranging in size from chickadees to condors nest in tree cavities. A few birds, such as kingfishers, puffins, and petrels, dig burrows to avoid predators. Larger species, such as Great Blue Herons, usually build their nests in the tops of trees, preferably on islands, where they are safest from such tree-climbing predators as raccoons. Some tropical birds locate their nests in the walls of the nests of stinging ants and wasps!

Least Terns dive at predators.

American Woodcock

Ground-nesting birds rely on camouflaged plumage.

Some birds nest in dense, thorny shrubs.

Northern Mockingbird

COLONIAL NESTING is the rule for seabirds. While land birds usually have large territories in which they collect food to raise their young, seabirds generally feed far from their nests and only defend the immediate nest site from neighbors in the colony. Bank Swallows and other colonial land birds that feed far from their nests select predator-safe habitats such as burrows in stream banks.

Colonial seabirds crowd together in part because safe nesting areas are often scarce, but colonial nesting also makes it easier to avoid predators since the whole colony watches for and chases them.

Colonial nesting also provides group stimulation and synchrony (events happening at the same time). In a colony, synchrony is important because it permits most of the eggs and young to be produced within a narrow time frame. This has the effect of swamping predators with large amounts of potential prey within a small period of time. Some eggs and young are usually taken by predators, but

Bank Swallows are among the few land birds that nest in colonies.

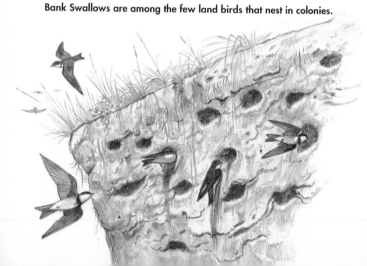

Common Terns are safer nesting in large colonies.

the losses are less when most of the eggs and young are produced over a short period. Colonial nesters also share information about the location of food supplies.

Colonial nesting does have disadvantages, however, for it creates stiff competition for nest sites within the colony. Often some members are forced to nest in marginal sites. Others may not be able to nest because of a scarcity of nesting sites, and sometimes it is difficult for birds to obtain ample nesting materials.

Other disadvantages include neighboring parents that sometimes attack young that wander outside of their own small nest site, as well as the increased risk of disease and parasites due to the crowded conditions. For seabirds, however, the benefits of colonial nesting far outweigh the problems, and 93 percent of them nest in colonies.

Blue-gray Gnatcatchers attach lichens to their nests.

NESTING MATERIALS tell a great deal about bird habits. Most land birds build the foundation of their nest from such coarse materials as sticks, bark, or plant fibers. Then they line the interior with down feathers, fine grasses, plant down, animal hair, or other soft material.

One study found that 78 percent of land-bird nests are lined with mammal hair. Green leaves are another frequently used lining. These may provide moisture during incubation and decrease the number of mites and other parasitic insects in the nest.

Some woodland birds, such as hummingbirds, the Blue-gray Gnatcatcher, and the Eastern Wood-Pewee, camouflage the exterior of their nests with large, leafy lichens secured with spider webs.

Birds that live near humans often incorporate plastics in their nests. Cormorants, for example, collect sections of lobster line and buoys, which they add to seaweed and

Bald Eagles may add to the same nest for 35 years.

other floating debris. In a similar way, many species use cellophane, candy wrappers, cigarette filters, letters, and plastics of various sizes, shapes, and colors. The Great Crested Flycatcher and other species that typically include the shed skins of snakes in their nests seem especially fond of cellophane and other transparent plastics. One Carolina Wren's nest was composed mostly of hairpins!

Bird nests are a tribute to avian industry. House Sparrows' nests, for example, may contain as many as 1,280 pieces of grass and feathers, and each item may represent an individual delivery. Barn Swallows may make 1,200 trips in order to deliver enough mud for their nests.

Most birds build new nests each year, but some large birds, like eagles and Ospreys, keep adding to their nests every year. Bald Eagles build the largest nests in North America, some reaching dimensions of 20 feet deep and 9.5 feet wide.

BIRDS BUILD THEIR NESTS by using their beak, feet, and breast. For most birds the beak is the main tool. It is used to break off branches or to pick up nesting material that is then carried to the nest. Some birds use their beak to weave materials into intricate forms, like the sacklike nests of orioles and the masterfully woven nests of weaver finches.

American Robins use their breast, legs, and beak to help fashion the interior of their mud-cup nest. When a female builds a new nest over a previous year's nest, she carries new mud (sometimes from distances a quarter of a mile away) and plasters this inside the old nest cup. Then she brings in grasses and drops them into the bottom of the nest. She sits in the nest, pressing her breast forward, while kicking backward with her feet and using her beak to tuck the grasses into the mud to form a soft grass lining.

African weavers construct elaborate nesting chambers.

Burrowing birds, such as puffins, petrels, and Burrowing Owls, first peck at the soil and then use their feet to excavate their deep burrows. Large birds, such as eagles and Ospreys, carry large branches in their feet, but feet are not nearly as important as beaks in nest building.

The length of time it takes to build a nest varies with the nest's size and complexity. Golden Eagles may require two months to build a nest, but since they reuse the nest with only minor patching each year, it may last their lifetime. Oropendolas, large tropical members of the blackbird family, spend three to four weeks building their 3-foot-long, pouchlike nest. In contrast, small land birds, such as Northern Cardinals, Gray Catbirds, and Northern Orioles, can usually complete their nest in less than a week. Mockingbirds are especially fast at nest-building and can often complete their nest in only one or two days.

Manx Shearwater digs burrow.

Robin builds mud-cup nest.

Chimney Swift glues twigs together with sticky saliva.

EGGS

Birds typically lay only a few eggs. They incubate the eggs and then feed and protect the young. This is in contrast to such egg layers as codfish, which may lay as many as 10 million eggs that are left at the mercy of the sea, or sea turtles, which may lay 100 eggs and then abandon them in a beach-sand nest.

FORMATION OF EGGS begins in a bird's ovary. Unlike most vertebrates (animals that have backbones), only the left ovary is functional in birds. The loss of the right ovary is probably associated with weight reduction for flight. The ovary of a two-week-old Red-winged Blackbird already contains about 100,000 oöcytes, the microscopic cells that develop into eggs. During the Red-wing's lifetime, only about 50 of these will mature to form eggs. The others are reabsorbed.

As day length increases, the size of the reproductive system greatly increases in both the male and the female. Courtship with a male and the longer days of spring and early summer stimulate females to produce higher levels of the hormone estrogen. This triggers ovulation—the rupturing of an ovum (yolk) from the ovary and the beginning of its descent down the oviduct. It then takes about 24 hours for the yolk to accumulate albumen (egg white) and a shell.

Fertilization occurs before the albumen and shell are added to the ovum. A sperm unites with an ovum soon after it enters the cup-shaped infundibulum at the top of the long, convoluted oviduct.

The next and longest section of the oviduct is the magnum. In most small- and medium-sized birds, the egg stays in the magnum for about three hours. During this time, most of the albumen is added. The albumen consists of about 88 percent water, 10 percent amino acids, and trace amounts of minerals. It keeps the embryo from drying out and helps to cushion the yolk.

In the isthmus, the developing egg receives the inner and outer shell membranes.

The hard outer shell is added in the uterus, where the egg spends its final 21 hours.

For most species, background color and markings are deposited during the last few hours in the uterus. The main factor determining whether an egg will have speckles, streaks, or squiggle markings seems to be the motion of the egg as it contacts pigment glands in the uterus. Pigment is often concentrated in a ring at the widest part of the egg.

Male Reproductive System

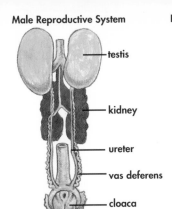

- testis
- kidney
- ureter
- vas deferens
- cloaca

Female Reproductive System

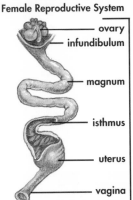

- ovary
- infundibulum
- magnum
- isthmus
- uterus
- vagina

oviduct

nonbreeding condition

breeding condition

The size of the reproductive organs increases dramatically as day length increases.

MOST BIRDS LAY THEIR EGGS early in the morning, after the shell has formed at night while the birds are quiet or sleeping. Some birds, such as the Ovenbird and the Cedar Waxwing, typically lay their eggs before sunrise. In contrast, some gulls and pheasants lay their eggs in the afternoon or evening.

Small perching birds, woodpeckers, and many ducks and geese usually lay one egg each day until their clutch is complete. Such larger birds as swans, herons, storks, and the Ostrich may take two days to form a new egg.

Once an egg is fully formed, the laying takes place rather quickly. Brown-headed Cowbirds and other brood-parasitic birds that lay their eggs in other birds' nests, for example, can lay their eggs in only a few seconds. A Northern Bobwhite, however, takes as long as ten minutes to lay an egg. Geese, turkeys, and other large birds may labor for an hour or longer to lay an egg.

In all birds, the pointed end of the egg usually emerges first.

EGG COLOR is believed to be a relatively recent development. Ancestral birds millions of years ago probably had white eggs, as do modern reptiles. The wide variety of egg colors in today's birds may be aids in preventing predation or in distinguishing eggs from those of neighbors.

Among living birds, white eggs are limited to cavity-nesting birds, to herons, doves, hummingbirds, nighthawks, and others that begin incubation immediately after their eggs are laid, and to ducks, geese, and others that cover their eggs with down each time they leave.

The Common Murre, a seabird that nests in crowded colonies but makes no nest, can recognize its own eggs by their characteristic pattern of squiggles. If the eggs from two females are exchanged, neither will incubate the mismatched eggs but instead begin immediately searching for their own.

In contrast, experiments have shown that many species, such as Herring Gulls, will incubate wooden eggs of varied sizes, colors, and shapes. Herring Gulls will even attempt to incubate rectangular or prism-shaped eggs, then reject them. This suggests that "feel" is as important as color.

Egg colors usually serve an adaptive function. The markings on Common Murre eggs below help each bird identify its own eggs.

MacGillivray's Warbler

Varied Thrush

Red-winged Blackbird

Gray Catbird

Lewis' Woodpecker

Pectoral Sandpiper

Least Tern

Anna's Hummingbird

Common Barn-Owl

Common Murre

EGG SIZE of no living bird equals the huge eggs of the now-extinct Elephant Bird of Madagascar. These big birds, which stood up to 10 feet tall, were exterminated by primitive humans, but shell remnants have been found measuring 13.5 inches long and 9.5 inches in diameter—large enough to hold about two gallons. This enormous egg contrasts dramatically with the 0.5-inch-long eggs of the tiny Vervain Hummingbird, which lives in Jamaica. The Elephant Bird's egg, which weighed about 18 pounds, was large enough to hold as many as 50,000 Vervain Hummingbird eggs!

Among living birds, the record for the largest egg goes to the Ostrich: about 6.8 inches long and 5.4 inches in diameter. Among flying birds, the Wandering Albatross lays the largest: 5.7 inches long and 3.5 inches in diameter. Eggs of the California Condor are a close second: 4.3 inches long and 2.6 inches in diameter.

Birds that have long incubation periods and hatch precocial, or well-developed, nestlings, such as chickens, ducks, and shorebirds, typically have larger eggs than do such birds as crows and herons that, in proportion to their size, lay small eggs. Their less-developed, or altricial, young spend a longer time in the nest.

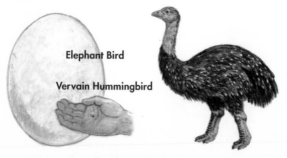

Elephant Bird

Vervain Hummingbird

Largest and smallest known bird eggs

Brown Pelican

Pelicans, cormorants, and boobies incubate their eggs under the warm webs of their feet.

BROOD PATCHES are bare areas on a bird's belly that are pressed against the eggs for incubation. During the breeding season, birds molt the down over the brood patch, and the blood vessels under the skin in this area become swollen. The warm blood circulated close to the skin of the patch keeps the egg or eggs warm.

In most land birds, only the female incubates the eggs, and the male does not develop a brood patch. In most shorebirds and seabirds, males share the incubation task, and so both male and female develop one or more brood patches. If the male does all of the incubating, as in Spotted Sandpipers, only the males develop brood patches.

Increasing day length triggers a rise in hormone levels. The hormones in turn trigger the molting of belly down to expose the brood patch and the underlying skin that is flushed with warm blood vessels. In contrast, ducks and geese do not molt their down but pluck it out and use it as a nest lining to keep their eggs warm. Some water birds, like gannets and pelicans, do not sacrifice the warm protection of their belly down but instead incubate their eggs under the webs of their feet, through which blood passes much as it does through a brood patch.

SIZE OF THE CLUTCH, or the number of eggs in a bird's nest, depends largely upon the amount and availability of food that the parent has for forming the eggs and then feeding the young. Gannets, puffins, petrels, albatrosses, and other seabirds that feed far from their nesting islands lay only one egg each year. In general, these parents have a high success rate in rearing their single young.

Quail, grouse, and ducks, in contrast, may lay ten or more eggs, and their precocial young begin feeding themselves soon after hatching. For these birds, the role of the parent shifts from that of food provider to that of guardian, providing protection from the weather and from predators. Because these birds do not nest in areas secure from predators as do seabirds that nest on remote islands, a higher percentage of young are lost to predators. The net production from their many-egg clutches may be no higher than that of island-nesting seabirds that lay only one egg.

The number of eggs birds typically lay in each clutch represents an attempt to produce the maximum number of young possible without decreasing the health conditions of either the young or the parents. Birds that lay only one egg usually live longer than do birds that produce large clutches. Some storm-petrels and puffins, as examples, often live for more than 20 years. Though they lay only one egg each year, they make up for this low production by producing young over many years and rearing them in protected burrows on remote islands.

Some species lay more eggs in years when food is more abundant. Hawks and owls, for example, generally lay a greater number in years of high rodent populations. This trend is especially noticeable in Snowy Owls that nest in the far north where there are large fluctuations in the numbers of lemmings, the small rodents that are their principal food. In years of peak lemming populations,

Gannets lay only one egg each year.

Ruffed Grouse lay large clutches.

Snowy Owls may lay twice as many eggs as in years when the lemming population is average. When the lemming population is at a low, the owls may not breed.

The length of the breeding season also influences the number of eggs laid. For example, resident or short-distance migrant land birds, such as American Robins and Mourning Doves, have two or more clutches each year .

Domestic chickens are well known for their ability to continue laying eggs as long as the eggs are removed soon after they are laid. This is called indeterminant laying, and it is a common trait of many wild birds. Flickers have laid as many as 71 eggs in 73 days in trying to build a clutch of 4 eggs.

Most birds, including such varied species as doves, shorebirds, and eagles, do not have the ability to produce eggs continuously. They are called determinate layers, and if part of the clutch is removed, they will usually continue to incubate the remaining egg or eggs without rebuilding the clutch. If an entire clutch is removed early in the season, determinate layers will generally lay a replacement clutch in a new nest built elsewhere in their nesting territory. If the eggs are lost late in the season, determinate layers usually abandon their nesting efforts for that season.

71

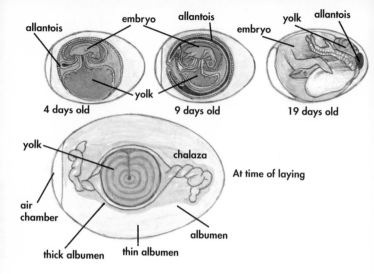

Lengthwise Sections of Domestic Chicken Eggs

INCUBATION in birds is similar to pregnancy in mammals. In both, this is a time when development of the young depends totally upon the parents, who provide warmth and protection for their growing young. In mammals, food and wastes are transported by the mother's blood, but in birds, the food is prepackaged in the form of the egg yolk. When a parent bird turns an egg, the chalaza suspends the yolk in the center of the egg. Body wastes from the growing embryo are accumulated as uric acid in the allantois, a large "bladder" at the egg's pointed end. Carbon dioxide, a product of embryo respiration, passes through the shell membranes and shell.

Usually both sexes incubate the eggs. Exceptions include those where one sex is conspicuously colored and the other

Northern Cardinal male feeds its mate on the nest.

has camouflaged plumage. In sexually dimorphic songbirds, the male spends more time defending the territory, while the female builds the nest.

Brightly colored male songbirds, such as tanagers and warblers, rarely sit on nests, but they often feed their somber-colored mates while they incubate. This enables the female to remain on the nest and permits more constant incubation. Such mate-feeding also serves to prepare the male for the pending task of collecting food for the young, and it also helps to reinforce the pair-bonding.

Among seabirds, the male usually shares equally in the incubating task. For seabirds that feed near their nesting islands, such as the Double-crested Cormorant, the parents may exchange places on the nest every one to three hours. For seabirds that feed far from their nesting colonies, incubation stints are much longer. Dark-rumped Petrels, as an example, incubate their egg for about 12 days before switching places with their mate.

EGG TEMPERATURE is controlled by the parents arranging their incubation stints so that the eggs are always tended. As an extreme case, Emperor Penguins are able to maintain their eggs at 93 degrees F for eight or nine weeks in the rigors of the Antarctic. The male accomplishes this by balancing the egg on top of his feet and pressing it up against his brood patch. He may transfer the egg from one foot to the other and even shuffle about in the colony, but he cannot let the egg slip off his foot while incubating.

At an opposite extreme, developing embryos of the little Fork-tailed Storm-petrel can tolerate cooling to 50 degrees F for as long as 28 days while the parents are away.

Embryos of the Common Murre, chickens, and probably many other birds make a variety of sounds inside the egg, but they have one particular sound that alerts the parents to resume incubation when the embryos become too cold.

EGG-TURNING may also help control egg temperature. Mallards turn their eggs every 40 minutes. American Redstarts and other small birds turn their eggs more frequently. The turning also prevents the embryo from sticking to the shell membrane.

OVERHEATING OF EGGS is a problem for birds nesting in hot, open places. Some tropical seabirds will stand over their eggs to shade them. Killdeers sometimes cool their eggs by first wetting their breast feathers and then dripping the water onto the eggs.

American Redstart turning eggs

Killdeer drips cooling water on eggs.

Kentucky Warbler

Downy Woodpecker

Ground-nesters have shorter incubation periods than cavity-nesters.

INCUBATION TIME depends upon the security of the nest site. Seabirds that nest on remote islands and particularly those that nest in underground burrows have very long incubation periods. Storm-petrels, for example, incubate their eggs for 38 to 56 days. Albatrosses hold the record, incubating their eggs for 81 days! As a general rule, the larger the bird, the longer its incubation period.

Land birds show a tendency for short incubation when their nests are vulnerable to predators. Thus, birds that build open-topped nests on the ground have the shortest incubation periods. In North America, cavity-nesting species have an average incubation period of nearly 14 days as opposed to open-nesting land birds, which have an average incubation period of 12 days. The parasitic Brown-headed Cowbird's egg has an incubation of only 11 days. This gives the young cowbird an edge over the nestlings with which it shares its foster home.

75

CARE OF YOUNG

HATCHING occurs when the young bird pierces its shell with its egg tooth, a horny growth at the tip of its bill. Young birds also have a strong muscle on the back of their neck. Called the hatching muscle, it gives them added power for breaking through the shell. This action, plus struggling and kicking, eventually frees the bird from its shell. Birds that hatch in open nests, like most sparrows and quail, can break out of their egg in a few minutes or within a day, but crevice-nesting birds, such as the Winter Wren, may take two or more days to break out.

BROODING is a transition period in which the parents keep the young warm, as they did in incubation. Young birds that develop downy plumages soon after hatching—grouse, pheasants, and shorebirds are examples—can maintain their own temperature within a few days, but birds that are naked at hatching, like chickadees and phoebes, cannot maintain their own body temperature until they are nine or ten days old.

FEEDING THE YOUNG is generally the responsibility of both parents. Yet precocial young, such as Killdeer and grouse, can start picking up food items of their own within hours of hatching. Altricial young are dependent upon their parents to provide food. Such young usually encourage parents to feed by opening their mouth wide while at the same time quivering their wings and uttering peculiar begging calls. The mouth lining of young altricial birds is usually brightly colored and often contains bright "targets" that elicit a feeding response from the parents. These targets and the color of the mouth lining fade as the young mature and become independent.

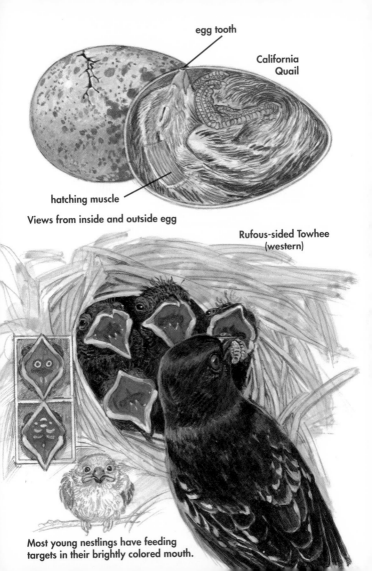

egg tooth

California Quail

hatching muscle

Views from inside and outside egg

Rufous-sided Towhee (western)

Most young nestlings have feeding targets in their brightly colored mouth.

KEEPING THE NEST CLEAN helps reduce the danger from predators and provides a healthy environment for the growing chicks. Young predatory birds, such as hawks and eagles, move back to the edge of their nest, raise their tail, bend forward, and shoot their excrement over the side of the nest. In a similar way, the young of birds that nest in barns, caves, sea cliffs, and similar predator-safe habitats also squirt their droppings over the side of the nest.

Most birds go to great lengths to remove excrement from the nest to keep the site clean and more difficult for predators to locate. Excrement of most small land birds is neatly sealed in a membrane known as a fecal sac. Many small land birds gently pull the fecal sac from their young. Eastern Bluebirds usually recycle nutrients in the excrement by swallowing the fecal sacs until the young are about six days old. After that age, the parents carry the sacs 20 to 50 yards away from the nest and drop them.

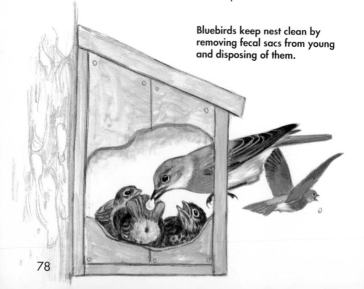

Bluebirds keep nest clean by removing fecal sacs from young and disposing of them.

Yellow-rumped Warbler

Most songbirds feed their young for at least a week after fledging.

WHEN YOUNG LEAVE the nest, they are usually as large as their parents. Occasionally, if they have had little exercise and plenty of food while in the nest, young birds may be even heavier than their parents. Most land birds, such as sparrows and warblers, stay with their parents for at least a week after fledging, or leaving the nest. During this time they are occasionally fed while they practice their own feeding skills. The young of Snow Geese and Whooping Cranes stay with their parents through their first winter migration, but many other water birds, such as cormorants, gannets, herons, and puffins, fledge without their parents and must find ample food and avoid predators by themselves.

Predatory birds such as certain hawks, owls, and terns feed their young for several months after fledging. This gives the young an opportunity to learn hunting skills while the parents supplement their meals. Frigatebirds may feed their single youngster for more than a year after it leaves the nest. Their habit of stealing food from other seabirds is a difficult feeding technique that requires considerable skill.

SONGS AND CALLS

Birds produce a remarkable variety of beautiful songs as well as peculiar buzzes, whistles, and chips. Most birds sing in the early morning, but some sing throughout the day. Others do not start performing until night.

BIRD SONG is a complex series of multiple notes produced in a recognizable pattern. When and how often birds sing is controlled by hormones. This links the main function of song to the breeding season.

Bird song functions mainly to establish and defend a nesting territory. For many species, song also helps to attract a mate. In many species only the males sing, and so the female may use a male's song as a measure of his experience. This may influence her choice of a mate.

Bobolink's high-pitched song has great carrying power over open habitats.

Blackburnian Warbler's song carries over forest canopy.

Forest birds, such as the Winter Wren, make their presence known with complex, beautiful songs.

HABITATS INFLUENCE the nature of bird song. Birds of open countrysides usually have high-pitched songs or buzzy sounds, accompanied by dramatic visual displays. Horned Larks, Bobolinks, meadowlarks, and woodcocks sing their high-pitched courtship songs in midair.

In contrast, forest birds, such as the Ruffed Grouse and owls, usually have low-pitched sounds that have greater carrying power through dense vegetation. Likewise, bitterns, rails, and other marsh birds that cannot perform visual displays due to the crowded marsh vegetation also have low-pitched voices.

Forest warblers, such as Blackburnian, Cape May, and Bay-breasted, have high-pitched songs that seem to contradict the rule that forest birds usually have complex, lower-frequency songs, but these warbler voices are useful for singing across the top of the forest canopy.

Both male and female Northern Orioles sing.

MALE SONGBIRDS do most of the singing. In the majority of species, males use song to establish the nesting territory and attract a mate. While males sing and actively defend the territory from intruding males, females do most of the incubation. In some species, however, females also sing. For example, female Northern Mockingbirds, Northern Cardinals, Northern Orioles, Rose-breasted Grosbeaks, Black-headed Grosbeaks, Pine Grosbeaks, and House Finches all sing songs that are as intricate as male songs. Females of other species, like Song Sparrows, sometimes sing in winter, but they leave all of the singing to the male once the breeding season starts.

Female songs may be especially helpful in alerting other females that the territory is occupied. Some studies have shown that female Northern Orioles will only chase other female orioles from their territory. Likewise, male orioles usually only chase other males.

American Robin

Brightness of sunlight determines time birds start singing.

THE DAILY PATTERN OF BIRD SONGS starts on early spring mornings when a predictable sequence of songsters begins the dawn chorus. Early in the breeding season, before the territory is well established and a mate attracted, many songbirds start singing as the sun rises and keep singing until dusk. As the nesting season advances and such responsibilities as incubation and feeding chicks take more time, the number of hours spent singing declines.

Bird song is usually most apparent in early morning. It typically declines by noon, then picks up again at dusk. Thrushes, such as the American Robin, Wood Thrush, and Veery, are notable dusk songsters. The midday slump corresponds with higher temperatures and greater winds, which interfere with carrying distance.

Sunlight determines the exact time a species starts to sing. On overcast days, for example, birds typically start singing a full hour later than they do on sunny mornings.

SEASON CHANGES influence the amount of singing, the length of the singing season, and the completeness of bird song. Experienced songbirds sing their most complete songs early in the breeding season when they are stalking and defending territories. The greatest frequency of songs occurs just prior to egg-laying. Males that do not attract mates will sing longer into the spring.

Male songbirds continue to sing through the incubation period, but the frequency of singing declines during incubation and may stop completely when the eggs hatch. If a pair re-nests after the first brood fledges, the frequency of song usually increases, followed by a decrease as the birds pass through the incubation and nestling period. In mid to late summer, after nesting, most adult songbirds molt their feathers and sing very little or not at all. As days shorten in the fall and day length approximates the shorter spring days, bird song may once again increase.

Male Common Yellowthroats sing less frequently after young hatch.

Gray Catbird

Many species produce whisper songs in severe weather.

WEATHER AFFECTS SINGING Birds do not like to sing in either rain or strong winds. Unusually cool weather may also reduce the amount of song or delay the time of day when birds start singing. In a similar way, intense heat at midday causes birds to seek shelter in shady places until temperatures improve. In contrast, humid weather may trigger vigorous singing and activity.

When it rains, some birds sing a whisper song that can be heard only at a distance of 20 yards or less. This quiet rendition is similar to the typical, or primary, songs and is often produced by both males and females when they are in concealed places such as interiors of shrubs and trees, where they seek shelter during weather extremes. Incubating birds may sing this song while sitting on eggs. Whisper songs are known from American Goldfinch, Rose-breasted Grosbeak, Gray Catbird, Warbling Vireo, Brown Thrasher, and many other songbirds.

CALLS While bird song is associated with territorial defense and the reproductive cycle, calls help birds to communicate about food and predators and with other members of their flock. Songs are complex, often musical; calls are usually short, nonmusical chips, chirps, squeaks, and squeals.

DISTRESS CALLS are sometimes given when a bird is captured by a cat, hawk, or other predator. These loud squeals may serve to distract the predator long enough to let the bird escape. Distress calls also attract other songbirds, which may start mobbing the predator. When parent birds hear distress calls from other birds, they often respond regardless of the species giving the call.

Distress call attracts other birds, which may mob a predator.

Birds harass a predator with scolding calls.

ALARM CALLS are given by both young and adult birds when they sight a predator. When a bird captured by a predator screams its distress call, the birds witnessing the event give excited chirp-and-squeak alarm calls. Such calls are similar in most land birds, making it easy for them to share information about predators. Such calls are typically short and have a wide frequency range, which makes locating the birds difficult. In addition to the excited chirps and squeaks, some birds give a scolding hiss sound that attracts other birds, which may mob the predator.

RALLY CALLS are given by a flock member after the group is dispersed by a predator. Northern Bobwhites, for example, live in flocks of about 20 birds. When threatened by a predator, they scatter in all directions, but the covey can quickly reassemble when one of the birds gives the rally call ("ka-loi-kee?-ka-loi-kee?"), a signal that the predator is no longer in the vicinity.

FLOCK CALLS help to maintain order in large bird assemblages. During the nonbreeding season, for example, several million blackbirds may sleep in a single huge roost. The sounds in such roosts are deafening, but they probably help to maintain individual space around a small section of a perch. The squabbling sounds help to remind neighbors to respect each individual's roosting space. In a similar way, shorebirds make high-pitched twittering sounds as they feed in great numbers on beaches and mudflats. These sounds encourage other shorebirds to keep out of an individual's private feeding space.

FLIGHT CALLS are high-pitched chips given during migration. They are especially apparent among such night migrants as warblers and thrushes, although many ducks and geese also give flight calls. Such calls are given by flock members within migrating flocks. They probably help birds to keep in contact with their neighbors while in flight and may decrease the chance of collisions with nearby members of the flock.

INDIVIDUAL RECOGNITION permits mated birds to coordinate their breeding behavior. It also allows young birds to recognize their parents' voices, which alerts them to feedings and dangers from predators. Paired Northern Ravens use specific calls to signal their mates—a behavior similar to our use of names. Such calls are apparently rare among birds, and only detailed studies can tease out such communication. Individual recognition is also important between parents and offspring. When gulls return to the nest with food for their young, they give a special call that signals the parents' own young to come forward for the feeding. Wood Duck chicks learn their mothers' voice while they are still in the egg.

Migrant birds maintain order in flocks by giving brief, high-pitched call notes.

Feeding territories among Semipalmated Sandpipers are maintained by a constant chatter of feeding calls.

HOW BIRDS SING AND CALL

Humans and other mammals produce vocal sounds by passing air over vocal chords in the larynx, an enlarged area located at the upper reaches of the trachea (windpipe). In contrast, birds produce their varied vocal sounds from the syrinx, which is located at the lower end of the trachea, where the bronchi from each lung join. Birds that lack the unique syrinx, like Turkey Vultures, are nearly silent, giving only an occasional hiss.

The boxlike syrinx holds elastic, resonating membranes and functions like a resonating chamber. The shape of the syrinx is modified by muscles that can stretch it in any direction to help modify the sound. These muscles determine the complexity of the song, and as a general rule, the more muscles attached to the syrinx, the more elaborate the song. Pigeons, for example, have only one set of syringeal muscles; more skilled songsters may have as many as nine sets of muscles.

Birds with the greatest carrying power, such as Whooping Cranes and Trumpeter Swans, have large windpipes. The Whooping Crane's 5-foot windpipe is mostly coiled inside the breastbone. A long windpipe acts as an air resonator to produce low-pitched sounds. Birds with short windpipes usually have high-pitched songs.

Some of the great bird songsters have two or more sets of vibrating membranes located inside and outside the syrinx. Not all bird sounds originate in the syrinx, however. Woodcocks, for example, have stiffened and narrow outer wing feathers. When wind passes through these feathers on the male's courtship flight ascent, they produce a pleasant, high-pitched twittering sound. Snipes use slotted tail feathers to make noise, while Ruffed Grouse compress air against their chest with their wings.

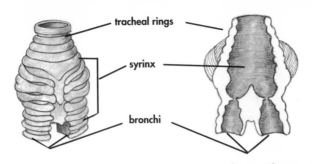

Bird vocalizations are produced in the syrinx as membranes vibrate.

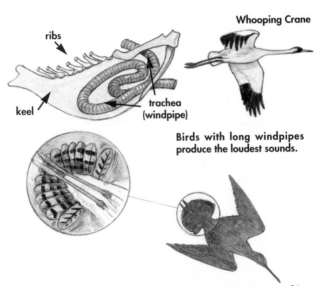

Whooping Crane

Birds with long windpipes produce the loudest sounds.

Some birds produce nonvocal sounds. Common Snipe in courtship flight lets wind stream through its tail feathers, making an eerie, throbbing sound.

DO BIRDS LEARN THEIR SONGS OR INHERIT THEM? Some birds develop songs and calls at the proper age without learning from parents or neighbors. Roosters start crowing and bobwhites give their loud territorial calls when they reach breeding age—even if they are reared in isolation. In a similar way, young Alder and Willow flycatchers reared in isolation will develop their songs in a normal way when they are old enough to sing. Completely inherited songs are rare in most songbirds, but even the most elaborate songsters have genetically determined call notes.

Most birds with complex songs, such as thrushes, wrens, sparrows, and finches, have a basic innate song pattern that is also greatly influenced by learning. Young finches and thrushes reared in isolation will develop a general song pattern, but it will not have distinct phrases. Young males will not develop songs like their father's unless they grow up hearing their father's or other males' songs.

DIALECTS are unique to birds and humans. Geographical barriers such as mountains, rivers, and grasslands isolate bird populations from each other. This leads to distinct dialects since young males hear only the songs from their father and there is little mixing between populations. If White-throated Sparrows are reared in isolation from their parents and hear tape recordings from distinct populations, they will learn these "foreign" dialects and retain them throughout their life.

Birds that have been isolated long enough develop such different dialects that they may not even recognize each other as belonging to the same species. Male Northern Cardinals vigorously defend their territory if they hear a playback of their own voice or that of a neighboring male. Cardinals in Ontario rarely respond to recordings of those from Ohio, however, and completely ignore those from Texas.

VOCAL MIMICS imitate other birds and a variety of sounds in their environment. Mockingbirds are the best-known mimics, but European Starlings, Blue Jays, Common Crows, Brown Thrashers, and many other species also mimic a few bird sounds.

Mockingbirds have imitated as many as 55 species in one hour! In addition to the calls of songbirds, their imitations include screaming eagles, crowing roosters, and even

White-crowned Sparrow

Young males typically learn to sing like their fathers.

the drumming of woodpeckers on metal roofs. They also imitate such non-bird sounds as creaking wheelbarrows, postmen's whistles, and barking dogs. Electronic comparisons show that these imitations are so accurate they cannot be distinguished from the actual sounds being imitated.

IMITATIONS, such as those of mockingbirds and other vocal mimics, are only one way to achieve a varied vocal repertoire. Some species achieve variety by producing many distinct phrases and mixing them in different sequences. In this way, Marsh Wrens can sing 210 different phrases in 45 minutes. Brown Thrashers, close relatives of mockingbirds, hold the record for varied phrases. They can sing 2,000 different phrases in an hour!

Varied songs seem to intimidate neighboring males more effectively than do less-varied songs. Apparently the listening attention of nearby males is greatest when songs pour forth with variety.

In many species, males accumulate more songs with age. Thus a variety of songs shows the age and experience of the male. Since experienced males are more capable of defending their territory and providing food for the female and the young, females probably benefit by selecting males with the largest song repertoire.

93

WHAT DO BIRDS HEAR?

Most bird song falls within 2,000 to 4,000 cycles per second (cps). This is slightly higher than the range used in human conversation. As a group, birds can hear sounds from .05 to 29,000 cps, while normal human hearing extends only from 50 to 16,000 cps. There is much variation from one bird to the next, however, and also some notable exceptions. Pigeons, for example, can hear extremely low frequencies of 0.05 cps, with an upper range of 7,500 cps. In contrast, the European Chaffinch can hear sounds within the range of 200 to 29,000 cps.

Face of Common Barn-Owl showing asymmetry of ear openings. Parabolic-shaped facial discs concentrate sound at the ear openings.

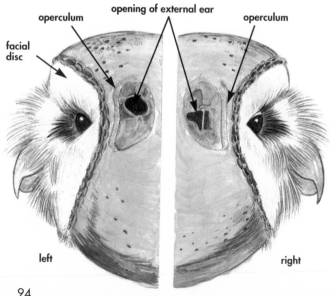

opening of external ear

operculum

operculum

facial disc

left

right

Environmental factors often affect a bird's hearing range. Great Horned Owls, as an example, often live in forests and have an extremely deep call of only 60 cps. This low frequency has great carrying power through dense vegetation. Yet Great Horned Owls can also hear sounds as high as 7,000 cps, and Long-eared Owls can hear sounds as high as 18,000 cps. These upper levels are probably useful because the owls feed on mice, which make high-pitched sounds.

Common Barn-Owls are especially adept at locating their prey by sound. Their disc-shaped face and the asymmetrical position of their ears help them locate and capture prey in total darkness. The disc-shaped face, much like a parabola, concentrates sound into the asymmetrically positioned ears. These help the owl to locate prey because sound reaches the two ears at slightly different times.

Most birds can receive sound signals throughout the body as well as through their ears. Sensitive feathers on the face, body, wings, and legs detect faint vibrations that help them find prey and avoid predators. These sound detectors are always turned on, ready to alert even sleeping birds of approaching danger. Birds can also separate sounds that arrive in rapid succession about ten times better than can humans, a talent that permits them to distinguish between very similar sounds.

HEARING RANGES

Species	Lower Limit (cps)	Upper Limit (cps)
Human	16	20,000
Mallard	300	8,000
Great Horned Owl	60	7,000
Long-eared Owl	100	18,000
Hairy Woodpecker	34	18,400
Pigeon	200	7,500
European Starling	100	16,000
European Chaffinch	200	29,000

BIRD FLIGHT

Nearly all birds can fly, and they master the sky with a grace and efficiency that humble human efforts. Much of the success of birds in the air is due to their marvelous and unique feathers. Studies of feathers and bird flight have made great contributions to our abilities to explore the air.

BIRDS HAVE MANY KINDS OF FEATHERS. The long flight feathers of the wings and tail are essential to bird flight. In order of their length and position on the wing, from the tip back to the body, the wing feathers, also known as remiges, are called primaries, secondaries, and tertials. The wing and tail feathers, called rectrices, are examples of contour feathers. They are the most visible type of feather. All of the surface feathers that cover the head, body, and legs are also contour feathers. These have in common a central shaft, or rachis, and a firm vane on either side of the shaft. Contour feathers are moved by a series of muscles attached to the feather follicle.

Semiplumes are fluffy feathers with a distinct rachis but a completely downy vane. These numerous, small white feathers are hidden beneath the body contour feathers. They fill in the form of the bird and also provide insulation and buoyancy, especially for water birds.

Down feathers are small, fluffy feathers found under the contour feathers on the body. They sometimes lack a rachis. Their main function is insulation, which explains why they are especially well developed in water birds.

Filoplumes are long, slender feathers that consist mainly of the long rachis. While some filoplumes have a small vane at their tip, others are completely hairlike and often extend beyond the contour feathers, especially on the neck and upper back. They function primarily to transfer vibrations to the skin.

Powder feathers are most pronounced in herons and certain hawks. They barely resemble other feather types. Only rarely do they have a feather quill, or calamus, and even when it exists, it is very small. In some species, the calamus barely protrudes through the skin. Constant shedding from the powder feathers gives a powdery blush to the plumage of certain birds.

Bristles grow almost exclusively on the head and neck. They resemble filoplumes, but they can be distinguished by their lack of barbs at the feather tip. Bristles that are located at the base of the bill, as in flycatchers and warblers, help birds detect the presence of flying insects. The facial bristles of owls, jays, and crows may enhance their sense of touch, as do the eyelash bristles of roadrunners and the Ostrich.

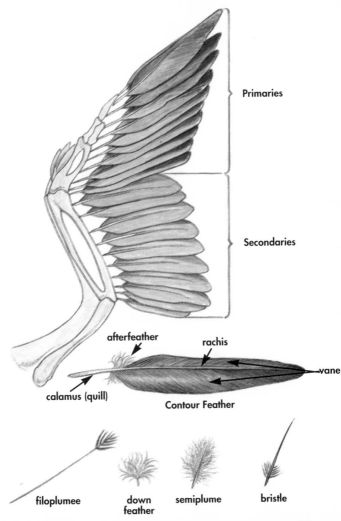

Primaries

Secondaries

afterfeather

rachis

vane

calamus (quill)

Contour Feather

filoplumee

down feather

semiplume

bristle

THE NUMBER OF FEATHERS on even a small bird is impressive. Tiny Ruby-throated Hummingbirds have nearly 1,000 feathers, while such large birds as Tundra Swans may have as many as 25,000. In proportion to their body weight, small birds have even more feathers than do large birds, for they have a greater need to conserve body heat. Birds that live in cold climates usually have more feathers in winter than in summer. House Sparrows, for example, have about 3,200 feathers in summer and about 3,600 in winter.

BIRDS MOLT worn feathers on a regular cycle and replace them with new feathers. Since feathers comprise 4 to 12 percent of a bird's body weight, it takes a great amount of energy to grow a replacement set. Timing of the molt must therefore occur at a season when food demands are low and food is abundant. For this reason, most birds molt their body and flight feathers in the fall after the nesting season when insects and fruits are abundant but before they begin their demanding southward migration. Some birds, such as ducks and warblers, acquire a drab body plumage in the fall, then molt a second time and replace this with bright feathers before the spring courtship season. Some sparrows, wrens, and ptarmigans may molt all of their feathers two or three times during the year due to excessive feather wear.

Birds molt their flight feathers in a predictable sequence. Most songbirds replace one primary at a time in each wing, starting at the wrist and then moving out toward the wing tip. After the primaries are replaced, the secondaries start molting in a paired manner, starting at both ends of the forearm and moving toward the center.

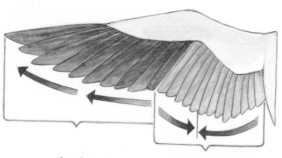

primaries

secondaries

FLIGHT PROBABLY ORIGINATED among the ancestors of modern birds when tree-dwelling reptiles began leaping from branch to branch. Such movements probably first led to soaring flight that developed later into flapping flight. Tree-climbing ancestral birds with feathers could fly faster and more dependably than could non-feathered reptiles. This helped the ancestral birds both in avoiding predators and in finding food.

Archaeopteryx, the oldest known bird, dates to about 140 million years ago. Its skeleton shows its close relationship to a small dinosaur—except that it has feathers. It probably had a cartilaginous keel on its breastbone, and this supported modest breast muscles. These did not permit it to make long migrations, but *Archaeopteryx* probably could fly through the trees using flapping flight.

Skeleton of *Archaeopteryx*

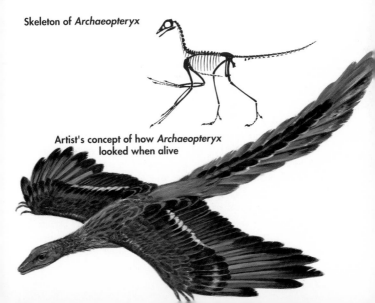

Artist's concept of how *Archaeopteryx* looked when alive

PRINCIPLES OF GLIDING FLIGHT are similar in birds and airplanes. The body and wings of both airplanes and birds show streamlining, which permits the wing to cut through the air with a minimum of drag.

When bird or airplane wings cut through the air, the action creates unequal pressure. Air must travel farther and hence faster over the curved upper side of the wing. This results in lower pressure since the air molecules are spread farther apart above the wing than below, where air speeds by the flat or concaved lower wing surface. Air molecules moving more slowly under the wing stay closer together, resulting in higher pressure. The difference in pressure creates lift. This effect is exaggerated in birds that have very convex upper wings and a strong concave shape to the underwing. Such highly cambered wings give many small forest birds the ability to gain elevation quickly.

Lift is further increased when the leading edge of the wing is tilted upward, thus increasing the angle of attack. When the angle of attack reaches about 15 degrees to the direction of the wing's motion in air, the airstream passing over the wing becomes turbulent, lift decreases, and a stall develops. Lift disappears at this stalling angle.

Birds that require great lift, like chickadees and other forest birds, increase their stalling angle by forcing a stream of air through several fingerlike feathers called the alula. These protrude from the wrist, creating wing slots that direct a stream of air close over the upper surface of the wing, and effectively reduce turbulence.

Large birds, like eagles and vultures, have wing slots between their primary feathers. Air that slips out from under the trailing edge of the wing tends to swirl upward and interferes with air moving over the wing. This turbulence creates drag and destroys lift. Such turbulence is especially great near the wing tip, where it is called the tip vortex. The extremely long wings of some seabirds, such as albatrosses, reduce this problem by moving the tip vortex far from the body.

Aspect ratio is the ratio of the length of the wing to its width. Long and narrow wings, like those of albatrosses, have an aspect ratio of 18:1 (for every inch of wing width, there are 18 inches of length). Such wings are so efficient that for every 40 grams of vertical lift, there is only 1 gram of resistance to forward motion.

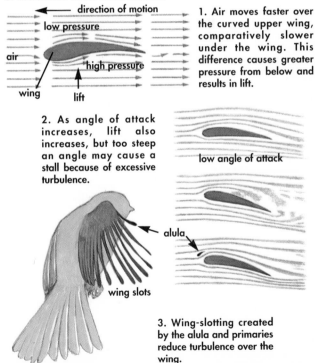

1. Air moves faster over the curved upper wing, comparatively slower under the wing. This difference causes greater pressure from below and results in lift.

2. As angle of attack increases, lift also increases, but too steep an angle may cause a stall because of excessive turbulence.

3. Wing-slotting created by the alula and primaries reduce turbulence over the wing.

Albatrosses are masters of dynamic soaring, capable of gliding 50 or 60 feet while losing only 3 feet of elevation.

Turkey Vultures ride a thermal, glide to find another, spiral up, and continue onward.

FLIGHT STYLES VARY. Whether birds glide, soar, or flap depends upon such factors as wing and body size and shape, available winds, habitat characteristics (such as forest, ocean, or meadow), perches, and predators.

Gliding is a common flight style for small to medium-sized ocean birds such as gulls and shearwaters. Gliding requires no forward propulsion and depends solely on the bird's body weight to overcome air resistance. When gliding, birds simply extend their wings and let gravity carry them forward.

Soaring birds can gain altitude without flapping their wings. Some accomplish this by static soaring, in which they climb on rising air currents known as thermals. Albatross wings are too long and narrow for static soaring. Instead, they practice dynamic soaring, in which they climb on layered air currents that are moving at different speeds.

Greater Shearwater

Flapping flight permits birds to become airborne.

Soaring birds, such as storks, vultures, and pelicans, must be able to withstand severe windstorms during their long migrations. Soaring land birds, such as hawks and eagles, stay aloft by riding thermals, which are hot-air columns that rise off mountains or from farm fields, airports, parking lots, or other flat areas. In thunderstorms, air may rise in thermals at the rate of 20 mph.

Soaring birds, like pelicans, storks, and vultures, typically have large, broad wings that permit them to ride the thermals. These birds also have conspicuous wing-slotting that increases lift.

All birds that fly do at least some flapping flight. Even the best gliding and soaring birds must gain elevation by flapping their wings. It is still unclear how birds use flapping to launch themselves into the air. Birds that depend on flapping have large, keeled breastbones that support their flight muscles. Such muscles may comprise 15 to 25 percent of a bird's body weight.

BIRDS DO NOT LEARN HOW TO FLY from their parents. Several researchers have demonstrated that bird flight is an instinctive behavior that emerges at the proper age without parental input. In one experiment, young pigeons were hand-reared inside narrow tubes that prevented the birds from opening their wings. After the young pigeons had grown all of their flight feathers, they were removed from the tubes and tossed into the air to see if they could fly. Not only did they take off in strong flight, but they flew just as well as pigeons of the same age that had been reared by parents.

While the outcome of the experiment might seem a surprise, many cavity-nesting birds, such as Tree Swallows and bluebirds, grow up in crowded conditions that parallel the confinement of the tube experiment. When young cavity-nesting birds fledge from their nest for the first time, they have had little chance to exercise their wings, but they can soon fly as well as their parents.

Young cavity-nesting birds usually fly on their first attempt.

Tree Swallows

Young Bald Eagles exercise their wings for several weeks.

Some burrow-nesting seabirds, such as puffins, start exercising their wings during the last week in their burrow and often come outside at night, when they are safe from predation by gulls, to exercise before heading to sea. Likewise, large birds of prey, such as eagles and the Osprey, will exercise their wings on the nest with considerable flapping.

The ability to have a successful first flight is especially important for cliff-nesting birds, such as eagles, Prairie Falcons, and kittiwakes. These birds nest in such precarious habitats that a "crash" on their first flight would probably make it their last flight.

Young birds must perfect their flying skills soon after leaving the nest so they can start finding their own food. Some parents fatten their young with enough extra food to permit them a few days or weeks to perfect these skills.

NAVIGATION AND MIGRATION

Each fall at least two thirds of the birds in North America make a migration of at least several hundred miles. Of these, at least 100 species leave North America to winter in tropical habitats south of the United States.

BIRDS MIGRATE to find ample food to power their rapid metabolism and to maintain their high body temperatures. Migration occurs among most birds that live in northern latitudes because food becomes scarce during winter.

Nearly all birds migrate from northern forests and tundra habitats in winter. Only 20 out of 215 breeding species, for example, spend the winter in Michigan. And only bark-feeding birds, such as nuthatches, chickadees,

Summer and winter areas used by migratory wood warblers, showing the much larger area occupied in summer.

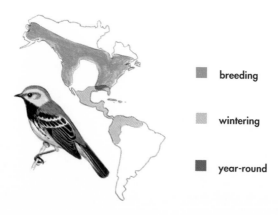

■ breeding

■ wintering

■ year-round

and woodpeckers, and seed-eating birds, such as cross-bills, siskins, and grosbeaks, typically winter in northern forests, where there is usually snow cover.

After birds complete their perilous journey to southern habitats, why do they bother to return north in the spring? Why risk the uncertainties of storms, predators, and accidents that they face when they leave the balmy tropics?

The answer to this question lies in the fact that northern habitats during spring and summer have an abundance of food in comparison to tropical habitats. When spring thaws unlock the northern lakes and forests, these habitats come alive with large numbers of insects, such as blackflies and mosquitoes, on which both young and adult birds can feed. During the long days of northern summers, migrant birds can rear more young than in the south.

Summer and winter areas used by eastern and western flycatchers, showing how they divide both their summer and winter ranges.

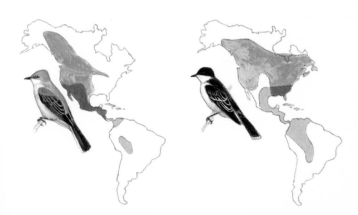

Most migrants show highly predictable migration timing. Cliff Swallows at San Juan Capistrano Mission are famous for their punctual return.

MIGRATION FACTS

THE TIMING OF MIGRATION is linked to the length of day. As day length increases with the advancing spring, birds develop a nocturnal restlessness called "zugunruhe." Increased exposure to daylight leads both males and females to higher hormone levels that trigger the urge to migrate. Migration becomes a predictable event. Cliff Swallows of San Juan Capistrano Mission in southern California and Turkey Vultures of Hinkley, Ohio, are noted for their punctual spring arrivals. The spring arrivals of many backyard birds such as American Robins and Red-winged Blackbirds are equally punctual.

NIGHT MIGRATION is the rule for most small, insect-eating birds, such as warblers, vireos, flycatchers, and thrushes. Some migrants use star patterns for orientation, but since they also migrate on overcast nights, there may be other reasons for nocturnal migration. Safety from predators, such as falcons, and water conservation are probably two of the main reasons so many migrants travel at night. In the cool night hours, birds lose less water from evaporation, enabling them to fly farther without stopping. During migration season, listen at night for the chirps and call notes of night migrants.

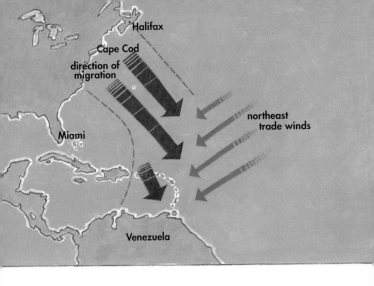

Many land birds migrate southeast from Cape Cod over Bermuda in a direction that would eventually take them to Africa. Trade winds, however, blow them back toward their winter homes.

MIGRATION ALTITUDES vary greatly between species and from one night to the next, but studies show most small birds migrate just below a mile in altitude. Spring migrants typically fly higher than fall migrants.

Radar studies have also shown that migrants fly higher late at night. Three to four hours after dusk, many migrants over Cape Cod, Massachusetts, flew 1,500 to 2,500 feet above the ground. Later at night, the same radar showed that migrants flew at 5,000 to 9,000 feet. On some nights, birds migrated nearly 3.5 miles high!

SPEED OF MIGRATION varies with the seasons. Spring migrants rush to breeding territories. Autumn migration goes more slowly.

Robins are relatively slow migrants, averaging about 37 miles per day. Some species show an increasing speed as they approach their summer territory. Blackpoll Warblers, for example, cover about 31 miles per day over most of their journey from Brazil to Canadian forests, but may clock 200 miles per day on the home stretch. With a strong tail wind, large waterfowl and wading birds may travel 500 to 1,000 miles in 24 hours.

HOMING ABILITY permits birds to travel to remote corners of the world and then return to familiar nesting areas. The homing ability of many birds is so well-developed that if they are blown far off course in storms or taken in experiments to regions far from their usual travels, they can often find their way home across unfamiliar territory.

A Manx Shearwater, for example, was removed from its burrow in Wales and flown 3,200 miles to Massachusetts, where it was released. Traveling a route it had never experienced before, it returned to its burrow in Wales 12.5 days later!

Some land birds can perform equally impressive homing. One researcher found that White-crowned Sparrows moved from California to Maryland could find their way home, a distance of 2,800 miles, within a year.

Many young birds, such as ducks and shorebirds, perform their first migration without assistance from their par-

Young Red Knots migrate without their parents.

Young puffins remember their way home after several years at sea.

ents. The urge to migrate during their first winter takes such birds from northern breeding ponds on treeless tundra habitat to tropical beaches and lagoons they have never visited previously. Such remarkable movements prove many young birds have a genetic map that permits them to travel between breeding and wintering homes without any help or experience.

Research with Atlantic Puffins in Maine and Collared Flycatchers in Germany has shown that nestling birds hand-reared at release sites distant from their original home will "imprint" to the release site. They apparently retain a mental map that permits them to return to the imprinted site several years later when they are old enough to breed.

Not all birds show such notable homing skills. Nonmigratory birds, such as titmice and certain wrens, often show little homing ability.

METHODS OF NAVIGATION VARY between species and perhaps even between individuals within the same species. Unraveling migration mysteries depends on discovering how birds navigate between their summer and winter homes. No one method is used by all species.

VISUAL LANDMARKS are the most obvious way of navigating. When viewed from the air, coastlines, rivers, and mountain ranges make up obvious patterns, most of which run in a north-south direction. Such landmarks may be especially important to hawks that migrate during daylight and use rising thermals from valleys and deflected winds off mountains to propel their soaring flight. Likewise, waterfowl often fly along coastlines and rivers where they land to rest and feed during migration. In a similar way, seabirds may use changes in water color to indicate water depth, or surface changes to indicate edges of ocean streams and currents. To date, however, there is little experimental evidence to show that migrants use any of these visual landmarks.

Although visual landmarks seem good guiding posts, it's apparent that birds must also have other navigation skills, since they often migrate at elevations well above cloud cover and even thick fog does not prevent them from finding their way home. Likewise, most small birds migrate at night when visual landmarks are probably difficult to see. For some birds, landmarks are part of a complex and redundant mix of navigation techniques.

Snow Geese may use familiar visual landmarks as they migrate down the Atlantic coast of the United States.

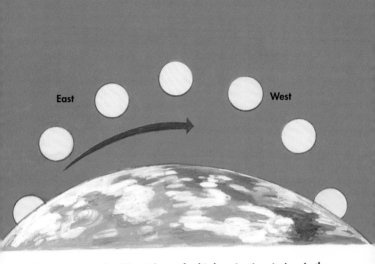

East   West

The sun is a predictable guidepost for bird navigation. It rises in the east and sets in the west, moving at the rate of about 15 degrees per hour.

THE SUN IS A LIKELY COMPASS for migrants because of its reliable and rhythmic regularity of rising in the east and setting in the west. Starlings placed inside circular cages, for example, will flutter in the appropriate direction for migration on sunny days but become confused on cloudy days.

Orientation using the sun as a compass also requires that birds have a sensitive biological clock keyed to the seasonal amount of light. The clock is necessary because the sun moves through the sky at the rate of 15 degrees per hour. Birds would have to adjust for this movement if they were attempting to fly in a straight line while using the sun as a compass. While some birds apparently do use a solar compass, it is clearly not their only navigation tool. The sun compass only helps birds to orient themselves when there is no cloud cover; it is useless to the majority of birds that migrate at night.

The sun undoubtedly helps some birds find their direction, but the sun compass alone cannot explain how birds find their way home from strange locations or how they compensate if they are blown off course. Obviously other navigational clues such as star patterns and magnetism are also important, especially for night migrants. The total explanation remains elusive.

STAR PATTERNS may serve as useful orientation points for such night migrants as warblers and finches.

Experiments in planetariums point to the importance of star patterns for nocturnal migrants. White-throated Sparrows captured during the spring migration and placed in a planetarium under the usual spring star patterns (the North Star in its proper location for spring), typically flutter in a northerly direction. When the planetarium sky showed the North Star in a southerly direction, however, the sparrows attempted to fly south.

Some researchers believe that nocturnal migrants use a "gestalt" configuration of stars as directional aids. The group of stars that rotate around the North Star are probably the most important.

THE EARTH'S MAGNETIC FIELD varies in strength, angle of dip, and direction (polarity) from one latitude to the next. Researchers have demonstrated that homing pigeons are very sensitive to this magnetic field. A tiny crystal of magnetite between their skull and brain may even serve as a compass.

Experiments have shown that when a magnet is attached to a homing pigeon's head it cannot find its way home. A nonmagnetic brass bar has no effect.

Research shows that Ring-billed Gulls, Indigo Buntings, European Robins, and Swainson's Thrushes are all sensitive to earth's magnetic field. Magnetic aids explain how birds can find their way on cloudy nights, in dense fog, or over trackless expanses of ocean.

tracks on blotting paper	drawings show orientation

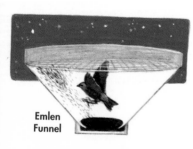

Emlen Funnel

Bird studies in planetariums often use the "Emlen funnel" to measure direction of nocturnal restlessness. Birds flutter up sides of a blotter-paper funnel, leaving tracks.

114

SOUND AND SMELL cues may also be important to bird navigation. Pigeons can hear sounds at a frequency as low as 0.05 cps, which is far below the human hearing range. These infrasounds are produced by such natural features as wind striking mountain ranges, surf pounding on beaches, and thunderstorms. Some birds can probably hear such sounds for hundreds of miles.

Leach's Storm-Petrels have a keen sense of smell. These nocturnal birds dig earthen burrows or nest in rock crevices on oceanic islands. They can return to their nesting islands in dense fog on inky black nights, apparently performing this remarkable navigation feat by smelling their nesting island. They also recognize their own nesting burrow by its distinctive odor.

NAVIGATION AIDS often interact, depending on circumstances. Birds need a variety of backup systems because they must cross varied terrains and go through changing weather conditions.

A pigeon flying home on a sunny day, for example, might use its sun compass to select a general direction, but if clouds roll in, it might shift to its magnetic compass. If the pigeon encounters magnetic anomalies, such as local iron deposits, it might be forced to take a major detour until its magnetic compass gives dependable signals. Some may use a sense of smell to correct their position, but on the home stretch rely on visual cues to find their familiar roost.

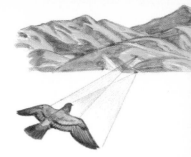

Pigeons can hear extremely low-frequency infrasounds and may use them to locate such landforms as mountains.

Leach's Storm-Petrels approach their nesting islands from an upwind direction. The pungent scent from their burrow guides them home.

115

BIRD POPULATIONS There are approximately 5 billion birds in North America during most of the year, and this number increases to about 6 billion immediately following the nesting season. There may be approximately 100 billion birds on earth, which is about 25 times more birds than people. Although some species are gravely threatened due to habitat loss, pollution, or other causes, most populations maintain their numbers with remarkable stability.

MOST YOUNG BIRDS DO NOT SURVIVE the first few months of life. If the majority of young survived, overcrowding and competition for food and nesting places would be severe. A detailed study of nesting Song Sparrows has shown that about 25 percent of every 100 eggs are lost to storms or to predators before they hatch. Of the remaining

74 nestlings, only 52 leave the nest, and 80 percent of these die during the first year. Only 10 adults remain to breed the following year. This study also found that 43 percent of one-year-olds die during their second year. This leaves just 6 birds from the 100 eggs to reproduce a second time.

HOW LONG DO BIRDS LIVE? If birds survive the first few years of life, they may live to surprising ages. Chickadees (which are nonmigratory) usually live only three years, but once they pass this age, they may live to six or more years. Likewise, resident birds of the tropics, such as tanagers and tropical thrushes, may live twice as long as migrants. In contrast, long-distance migrants, such as North American warblers, usually live only a few years. Larger birds tend to live longer.

MAXIMUM KNOWN AGES OF BANDED WILD BIRDS

SPECIES	AGE (YEARS)	SPECIES	AGE (YEARS)
Yellow-eyed Penguin	18	Evening Grosbeak	13
Red-throated Loon	23	Golden Eagle	25
Laysan Albatross	42	Osprey	32
Short-tailed Shearwater	30	Peregrine Falcon	14
Brown Pelican	31	Wild Turkey	12
Double-crested Cormorant	23	American Coot	19
Great Frigatebird	34	American Oystercatcher	36
White Stork	26	White-breasted Nuthatch	9
Trumpeter Swan	24	Purple Martin	8
Canada Goose	23	Herring Gull	32
Mallard	29	Arctic Tern	34
Blue Jay	15	Atlantic Puffin	21

100 eggs of Song Sparrows

74 live nestlings

52 fledglings

1 year later — 10 birds reach breeding age

2 years — 6 birds left

3 years — 3 left

4 years — 2 live to be 4 years old

Fate of 100 Song Sparrow Eggs

SPECIES	AGE (YEARS)	SPECIES	AGE (YEARS)
Common Barn-Owl	18	European Robin	11
Eastern Phoebe	9	Black-and-white Warbler	11
Ruby-throated Hummingbird	5	European Starling	20
Red-bellied Woodpecker	20	Red-winged Blackbird	14
Barn Swallow	16	Purple Grackle	16
American Crow	14	Scarlet Tanager	9
Summer Tanager	6	House Sparrow	10
European Jay	16	Northern Cardinal	13
Black-capped Chickadee	12	Dark-eyed Junco	11
House Wren	7	White-crowned Sparrow	13
American Robin	11	Song Sparrow	10

PREDATORS, such as hawks, snakes, and foxes, help to keep bird populations stable, but predators have relatively little effect when compared to losses from starvation, accidents, inclement weather, disease, and parasites. Such large predatory birds as gulls, eagles, and certain hawks and owls have few predators except humans.

Young, inexperienced birds that have just left the nest are the most vulnerable to predators because fledglings are neither as fast nor as wary as adults.

Predators influence every feature of a bird's appearance and behavior, but the influence of predators is especially apparent at the nest. For example, birds avoid predators at their nests by either hiding the location of the nest or by placing the nest in an inaccessible location, such as a tree cavity, cliff face, or deep burrow. If the eggs are exposed to view, they are usually speckled with markings that help them blend into their habitat. Likewise, young birds reared in predator-exposed habitats generally have cryptic markings, which are lacking in related species nesting in predator-free habitats.

Kittiwake chick, conspicuously marked

Cryptically colored Herring Gull chick

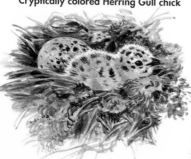

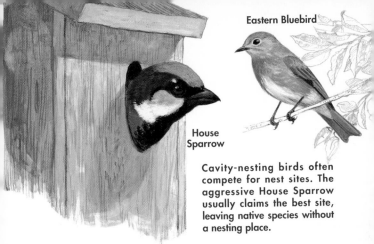

Eastern Bluebird

House Sparrow

Cavity-nesting birds often compete for nest sites. The aggressive House Sparrow usually claims the best site, leaving native species without a nesting place.

COMPETITORS reduce populations of similar species by competing for food and nesting places. This effect is usually minimal for similar species that have coexisted for many generations, but it can be severe for species whose ranges have recently overlapped. Similar species that overlap in range and habitat usually have sufficient differences in feeding habits and in nesting arrangements, and thus competition is reduced. Yet many species actively compete, especially for nesting places. The limited number of tree cavities, for example, usually limits the population of cavity-nesting birds, such as bluebirds, House Wrens, and Tree Swallows. Since nesting places are scarce for these species, a population decline for one cavity-nester can produce a population increase in another.

Competition for nesting places is especially acute when introduced species such as the House Sparrow and the European Starling compete for cavities with native birds such as bluebirds and Tree Swallows. The native birds have not developed appropriate competitive adaptations.

119

Sandhill Cranes

Sudden hailstorms can knock large birds from the sky.

DISEASES AND PARASITES are common in wild-bird populations, but because birds often show no symptoms, the disease or parasite condition is difficult to detect. A close examination of bird feathers usually shows some feather lice and mites. These are harmless in small numbers, but large numbers can be fatal. Birds may also carry various viruses and protozoa in their blood. Avian malaria is probably the most common blood disease, with mortality rates as high as 90 percent.

Diseases can sometimes be a major factor lowering bird populations, especially when birds are crowded during times of food shortage or drought. In an outbreak of botulism, for example, the bacterium *Clostridium botulinum* killed 250,000 ducks at Great Salt Lake in 1932. Likewise, the mold *Aspergillus* killed 2,000 Canada Geese at a Missouri wildlife refuge in 1966, and a flagellated protozoan, *Trichomonas gallinae*, led to the death of about 25,000 Mourning Doves in Alabama in 1951.

WEATHER AND ACCIDENTS can devastate bird populations. Migratory birds are especially vulnerable to such disasters, since unpredictable winds and storms can interrupt migration and force birds into habitats where they have little chance of survival. Hailstorms are especially destructive. For example, two hailstorms in Alberta, Canada, in July of 1953 killed over 148,000 waterfowl. Likewise, a 30-minute hailstorm in New Mexico killed 1,000 Lesser Sandhill Cranes. Birds that migrate over large lakes and oceans are especially vulnerable. A severe spring storm in the Aleutian Islands lasting five days killed more than 100,000 murres.

Early spring migrants are experts at finding insects even in cold weather, but late-spring snowstorms can destroy populations of most insect-eating migrants, such as Scarlet Tanagers and Purple Martins. Such storms often lead to widespread starvation when cold temperatures numb flying insects and delay the hatching of insect broods.

Late-spring snowstorms can devastate insect-eating migrants.

Scarlet Tanager

CONSERVATION

The number and variety of birds that live in a given area can indicate the health of the habitat. This relationship holds because birds require large amounts of nutrient-rich food, and such food supplies exist only in healthy habitats. If an area becomes degraded by toxic wastes from oil spills, pesticides, acid rain, or other forms of air, water, or land pollution, the absence of birds will be one of the first warnings that the habitat is also unsafe for humans.

HABITAT LOSS is the most destructive blow humans level at birds. All birds need food, water, nesting sites, and shelter. In addition, each species has its own list of specific habitat requirements. Some birds, such as European Starlings, are very adaptable and can live in a wide variety of habitats, but most species are much more selective. If a habitat is bulldozed, drained, eroded, or poisoned, the variety of plants and animals will decline.

WETLANDS are the marshes, ponds, swamps, estuaries, and other shallow-water regions along our coasts and inland waters. Shallow water is especially productive, since abundant sunlight permits vegetation to flourish, and this feeds a myriad of animals on which birds feed.

There were about 92 million acres of wetlands remaining in the lower 48 states in 1990. Although this represents only 5 percent of the country's land area, a third of all the birds in North America occur in wetland areas. Yet wetlands are being converted to farmland, housing developments, and parking lots at the rate of about 500,000 acres every year.

FARMLAND can be excellent bird habitat. Modern farming practices favoring large, single-crop farms instead of small, multi-crop family farms have, however, removed much previously good upland habitat. Small farms often maintain hedgerows to separate property lines and preserve wet areas and woodlots. These features have disappeared in many areas.

Abundant use of pesticides and herbicides offers temporary crop-production benefits but reduces the variety of insects and weed seeds.

Tropical forests are disappearing throughout the world at a rapid rate as roving farmers burn ancient forests, farm for a few years, and then abandon the depleted land to repeat the cycle elsewhere.

TEMPERATE FORESTS near urban areas are rapidly falling to house our expanding population. New subdivisions, shopping centers, power lines, roads, and highways remove forested habitats and fragment once-large woodlands.

Several recent studies have shown that birds nesting in the interior of such forests often disappear as the size of the woodland decreases. Such species as the Scarlet Tanager, Ovenbird, Red-eyed Vireo, and Barred Owl require a complete forest structure with many layers for singing, nesting, and feeding.

TROPICAL FORESTS are the winter home for 107 species of migratory land birds from North America. They cover only about 7 percent of the earth's surface, but are home to about 50 percent of all plants and animals.

Tropical forests are being degraded at the rate of about 62,000 square miles each year, an area the size of West Virginia. Tropical-forest conservation is vital to protect the winter homes of North American migrants and the many resident plants and animals and to preserve these species-rich forests.

HABITAT QUALITY insures that a protected habitat is not degraded in subtle ways. Protecting wetlands by posting them as wildlife sanctuaries, for example, accomplishes little if toxic chemicals drained from surrounding lands cause the water quality to deteriorate. The loss of complete habitats, such as in drained wetlands and logged forests, has an immediate and dramatic impact on wildlife. Slow degradation of habitats by poisoning or climate change can have an effect at a regional or even global scale.

WATER POLLUTION occurs when fertilizers and pesticides run into rivers and marshes. Likewise, irrigation water may accumulate natural elements such as selenium that can poison wildlife. Each year 543 billion pounds of toxic waste are generated in the United States from the manufacture of such items as paints, plastics, and household chemicals. Of this amount, about 135 billion pounds are released into rivers, lakes, and streams.

LEAD POISONING results when birds swallow lead, such as shotgun pellets or fishing weights. These pellets are usually picked up by ducks and geese along with the gravel used to crush seeds. They are responsible for the deaths of an estimated 1.6 million waterfowl every year. Condors, vultures, eagles, and other land birds that scavenge on game animals are also poisoned. Steel shot is an alternative to lead shot, now illegal.

Some wetlands have up to 120,000 lead pellets per acre.

124

Laysan Albatross

Plastics dumped at sea are often consumed by seabirds.

PLASTICS, such as plastic bags, are often swallowed by albatrosses, sea turtles, fish, and marine mammals, which may mistake them for jellyfish. Ingested plastics may block the digestive tract, give a false feeling of satiation, or cause ulcers.

MONOFILAMENT FISHING LINE from anglers entangles many fish-eating birds that break lines and later tangle the line around their wings or around a tree or other snag. Pelicans, herons, gulls, and terns are especially vulnerable. Monofilament fishing nets also take a huge incidental catch of seabirds. Diving seabirds, such as murres and puffins, can not see the net, they become entangled, and some drown.

OVERFISHED stocks of marine fishes can have devastating effects on seabird populations. Efficient, modern methods of capturing fish can crop 50 to 70 percent of available fish for human consumption, leaving little for fish-eating birds.

OIL tankers lose about 2 to 5 million tons of oil at sea every year. Most of this is not lost in the super spills that make newspaper headlines, but rather through the routine rinsing of storage tanks while ships are at sea. Oil kills seabirds by matting the feathers and by breaking the feather waterproofing. When seabirds attempt to clean oil from their feathers, they may ingest some of the oil, which leads to stomach ulcers.

125

CLIMATE CHANGE resulting from human activities threatens to have a profound impact on all plants and animals. If predictions about climate change prove accurate, most bird populations will suffer. Birds are very sensitive to rapid changes in food supplies and specific habitats.

WHEN FOSSIL FUELS, such as gasoline and coal, are burned, they release carbon dioxide (CO_2). This rises in the atmosphere and creates a shield that blocks some of the sun's heat close to the earth, much like glass traps heat in a greenhouse. Predictions are that this greenhouse effect may raise the earth's temperature by an average of at least 10 degrees F within the next 100 years. While about 75 percent of this CO_2 comes from auto exhaust and power plants, burning tropical rain forests are also a major source. Burning forests bring about a double loss in air quality, since living trees cleanse the air of CO_2. If predictions are correct, vast numbers of northern trees will die and southern trees will not be able to "move northward" fast enough to keep pace. Most birds will probably not be able to adapt to such rapid changes.

SEA LEVELS HAVE ALREADY RISEN 4 to 6 inches during this past century, and the amount of increase will accelerate with global warming. Sea levels rise because warm water expands and because polar ice caps melt. This flooding will not only impact major coastal cities but also vastly affect the present distribution of precious wetlands and nesting islands used by coastal birds. By the end of the next century, the oceans may have risen by 6 feet, enough to flood many coastal cities and wetlands.

OZONE DEPLETION in the stratosphere results when human-produced chemicals drift into the stratosphere and destroy the protective layer of ozone that shelters the earth from searing ultraviolet radiation. Chlorofluorocarbons (CFCs) are especially destructive to ozone. CFCs are used as refrigerator and air-conditioner coolants, in spray-can propellants, and in the manufacture of foam pillows and styrofoam cups. When a CFC molecule breaks loose from earth, it slowly drifts upward to the stratosphere, where ultraviolet radiation shatters the molecule and releases chlorine. One atom of chlorine destroys about 100,000 molecules of ozone. This effect has already led to a global loss of 3 to 5 percent of the earth's ozone.

In Antarctica, up to 50 percent of the stratospheric ozone is lost in some years. Without the protective ozone, ultraviolet radiation will kill abundant plankton living at the ocean surface. Plankton forms the

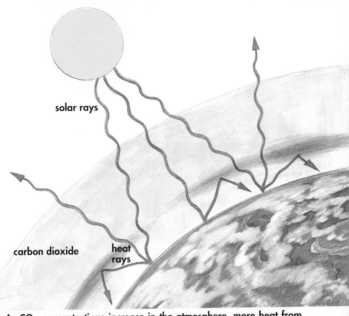

labels: solar rays · carbon dioxide · heat rays

As CO_2 concentrations increase in the atmosphere, more heat from the sun is trapped close to the earth. This greenhouse effect leads to global warming.

base for marine ecosystems and provides most of the new oxygen in the atmosphere.

ACID PRECIPITATION results when coal and oil are burned at power plants and factories. Sulphur and nitrogen are converted in the atmosphere to acids that fall with rain, snow, and fog onto vegetation and lakes as far as hundreds of miles downwind from the pollution source. Many trees in northeastern United States and Canada have already been weakened by higher soil acidity. Acid precipitation also causes the release of poisonous metals from soils. The loss of trees in forests degraded by acid precipitation means less food for caterpillars and other leaf-eating insects that nourish many of the northern warblers and other forest birds. Fish-eating birds, such as loons and mergansers, are also affected because the acidic water in many northern lakes has killed fish and crustaceans on which they feed.

127

WHAT IS BEING DONE to help wild birds? While the problems facing wildlife (and the quality of human life) are immense, there is abundant evidence that we can find solutions to environmental problems. Prior to 1900, for example, there were few protective laws or wildlife sanctuaries, and most birds were hunted extensively for food and feathers. Even such songbirds as robins, warblers, and hummingbirds were frequently used to decorate hats, and most wild species were readily available at food markets. The outrage of concerned people, however, stopped this slaughter.

This grassroots awakening has continued to grow and has the potential to solve the conservation problems that currently threaten wild birds. People *can* solve environmental problems as well as create them. Here are some encouraging examples.

WILDLIFE LEGISLATION now protects all birds in North America except the introduced European Starling, House Sparrow, and Rock Dove. A Convention for the Protection of Migratory Birds was signed in 1916 by the United States and England (representing Canada). This marked the beginning of federal regulation of game birds and prohibited the hunting of all other birds. The federal government later signed similar bird-protection treaties with Mexico in 1936, with Japan in 1972, and with the Soviet Union in 1976. These laws now protect 816 species of North American birds on their summer and winter ranges. It is illegal to possess these species or their feathers, parts, eggs, or nests without special federal and state permits.

SPECIFIC LEGAL ACTIONS by the federal government are working to help wild birds. In 1972, for example, the Environmental Protection Agency outlawed the use of DDT in the United States. This insecticide had led to population declines of the Osprey, Bald Eagle, Peregrine Falcon, and many songbirds. Since the outlawing of DDT, most Osprey and Bald Eagle populations have shown significant increases.

In a similar effort to help wild birds, the U.S. Fish and Wildlife Service adopted a plan to phase out the use of poisonous lead shot used by hunters and to replace this lead shot with nontoxic steel shot. The phaseout, which started with the 1987-1988 hunting season, was scheduled for completion in 1991.

The National Wildlife Refuge system manages 88 million acres of wildlife habitat in 425 units throughout the United States.

NATIONAL WILDLIFE REFUGES had their beginning in 1903 when President Theodore Roosevelt issued an executive order that protected Pelican Island off the east coast of Florida as "a preserve and breeding ground for native birds." Roosevelt created 52 additional refuges before leaving office in 1909. In 1929, following a decade of drought and declining wildlife, Congress passed the Migratory Bird Conservation Act authorizing the creation of migratory-bird refuges.

The National Wildlife Refuge System has grown to include 425 units encompassing 88 million acres, 77 million in Alaska.

The National Wildlife Refuges offer breeding, migration, and wintering habitat to many kinds of wildlife. Since most refuges were established to protect migratory waterfowl, such as ducks and geese, they also protect habitat for other water birds such as herons, ibis, cranes, and rails. Many refuges welcome human visitors.

PRIVATE CONSERVATION ORGANIZATIONS play a vital role in protecting wild birds. Even before the federal and state governments began efforts to protect birds with legislation and wildlife sanctuaries, concerned people were organizing groups dedicated to protecting wild birds and their habitats. Private conservation organizations serve as watchdogs over state and federal agencies and promote legislation and programs that benefit wildlife and natural habitats. They also identify conservation issues and encourage members to urge elected representatives to vote for pro-environment legislation. In North America, about 25 organizations are primarily concerned with bird conservation. In addition, several hundred groups are concerned with conservation of natural resources. Described here are four of the largest, most active groups. (Also see p. 156.)

NATIONAL AUDUBON SOCIETY conducts scientific studies of bird-conservation issues and actively promotes conservation legislation and education. The society has more than 500,000 members organized into more than 500 chapters throughout North America. It keeps its members informed about environmental issues by publishing *Audubon*, *American Birds*, and *Audubon Activist*. It also has a natural-history program for schools called "Audubon Adventures."

Founded in the early 1900s, it led the battle to end the slaughter of birds for the millinery (feather) trade. Today it protects 70 wildlife sanctuaries, most of which are important breeding areas for colonial water birds, and it operates resident Environmental Education Camps and Centers for children and adults. For more information contact National Audubon Society, 950 Third Avenue, New York, NY 10022.

WORLD WILDLIFE FUND–U.S. works worldwide to protect endangered wildlife and wildlands, especially in the tropical forests. World Wildlife Fund has helped establish 180 national parks and nature reserves, supports scientific investigations, monitors international trade in wildlife, and assists local groups in conservation projects. World Wildlife Fund–U.S. publishes a monthly membership newsletter *Focus*. The organization was formed in 1961 and has about 300,000 members. Contact World Wildlife Fund–U.S., 1250 24th Street, NW, Washington, DC 20037.

An Audubon trip to observe birds in their natural habitats

NATIONAL WILDLIFE FEDERATION educates people about the need for wise use and proper management of natural resources. It accomplishes this through a wide variety of publications, including *National Wildlife*, *International Wildlife*, and two children's magazines, *Ranger Rick* and *Your Big Backyard*. It also publishes an annual *Conservation Directory*, a comprehensive list of conservation organizations and environmental leaders. In addition, NWF sponsors week-long Conservation Summits that focus on the natural history and conservation of various regions. It also litigates environmental disputes. Organized in 1936, NWF has 4,800,000 members, with affiliate organizations in every state and a network of 13 regional offices. Contact National Wildlife Federation, 1412 16th Street, NW, Washington, DC 20036-2266.

THE NATURE CONSERVANCY is an international membership organization dedicated to acquiring land with unusual natural features or exceptionally high biological diversity. Its mission is to find, protect, and maintain the best examples of ecological communities, ecosystems, and endangered species throughout the world. Since it was founded in 1951, it has been responsible for the protection of nearly 3.5 million acres in 50 states, Canada, Latin America, and the Caribbean. Some lands are transferred for management to other organizations, but its system of some 1,000 preserves is the largest privately owned nature-preserve system in the world. It publishes *The Nature Conservancy* magazine for its 343,000 members. Contact The Nature Conservancy, Suite 800, 1800 N. Kent Street, Arlington, VA 22209.

131

WILDLIFE SUCCESS STORIES offer hope that with enough planning, financial support, and persistence, some species can be rescued even from imminent extinction.

TRUMPETER SWANS have a wingspan of up to 8 feet and hold the record as the heaviest flying bird in North America. They were once widespread and abundant in Canada and northern United States, but overhunting for food and for their dense feathers (used in comforters and powder puffs) nearly led to their extinction. By 1932, only 69 Trumpeter Swans survived in the lower U.S. on several isolated lakes near Yellowstone National Park. The U.S. Fish and Wildlife Service protected these survivors and moved some to other areas within their historic range. These actions led to a dramatic recovery. The Trumpeter Swan population has now increased to about 5,000 birds. For more information contact The Trumpeter Swan Society, 3800 County Road 24, Maple Plain, MN 55379.

WHOOPING CRANES numbered approximately 700 in 1870, but intense hunting and the draining of wetlands along their migratory route nearly led to their extinction. By 1941, only 15 birds survived in the wild. Since that low point, protection from hunting and an egg-transfer program have greatly improved their prospects for survival. By 1985, there were 28 pairs nesting at Wood Buffalo National Park in Alberta, Canada. These adults and their young numbered 120 in 1988. In addition, another Whooping Crane population, containing about 30 to 35 birds in 1986, was started at Grays Lake National Wildlife Refuge in southeastern Idaho. Sandhill Cranes served as foster parents. For more information write International Crane Foundation, E-11376 Shady Lane Road, Baraboo, WI 53913-9778.

Young Whooping Crane with foster-parent Sandhill Cranes

Hunting and the draining of wetlands caused the Whooping Crane population to plummet to only 15 by 1941. An egg-transfer program in which Sandhill Cranes serve as foster parents has led to a second wild population in the Rockies.

PEREGRINE FALCON populations were decimated in most parts of North America by the widespread use of DDT and similar pesticides after World War II. The poisons caused the birds' egg shells to become thin so that the eggs were usually crushed by the incubating parents.

The banning of DDT in 1972 resulted in normal egg shells in some areas, but elsewhere shells remain thin. This suggests that some Peregrines are still picking up DDT on their winter range. Brazil, for example, used 30,000 metric tons of DDT in 1984. Captive rearing programs, in which birds are hatched in captivity and then "hacked" from exposed platforms where they receive food through a hidden chute, have proved very successful. By 1990, there were 84 pairs established on territories from North Carolina to Maine. Contact The Peregrine Fund, Inc., 5666 West Flying Hawk Lane, Boise, ID 83709.

Peregrine Falcon

Hacking programs in large cities are fledging young falcons.

Atlantic Puffin

Decoys have helped to lure adult puffins back to Eastern Egg Rock.

ATLANTIC PUFFINS were hunted along the Maine coast for food and feathers in the late 1800s, which nearly led to their extinction in this region. The National Audubon Society and the Canadian Wildlife Service are working to restore puffins to some of their historic nesting islands off the Maine coast. Between 1973 and 1981 these organizations transplanted 734 two-week-old puffins from the large colony on Great Island, Newfoundland, to Eastern Egg Rock, a former nesting colony off mid-coast Maine. These chicks were hand-reared in artificial burrows, banded, and then released. Five pairs returned to breed at the island in 1981, and the colony had grown to 15 pairs by 1990.

National Audubon has used similar techniques to restore colonies of terns and storm-petrels to the Maine coast. Write Project Puffin, National Audubon Society, 159 Sapsucker Woods Road, Ithaca, New York 14850.

135

WHAT YOU CAN DO The problems that face birds and other wildlife are largely a result of human lifestyles and rapid population growth.

While new technologies have brought us a more comfortable and productive life, they have also given us such unforeseen problems as acid precipitation and the greenhouse effect, which threaten all life on earth. Here are some actions you can follow to help assure future generations a chance to enjoy the birds we know today:

Join a conservation organization to stay informed about issues (see pp.130-131 and 156).

Write letters to your elected representatives to make your opinions on conservation issues known.

Be a conservation-wise consumer. As an example, avoid fast-food beef that was produced in tropical countries, for this is often a product of pastures where rain forests were burned. Also, think efficiency. Each light you turn off in a room reduces oil pollution in the seas, acid rain, and greenhouse gases. Buy products packaged in recyclable paper or plastic. Recycle paper, cans, glass, and plastic. Start a backyard compost heap. Small daily actions can collectively make a huge difference.

Participate in such bird-monitoring programs as the Christmas Bird Count, wherein observers census the number of birds within a 15-mile-diameter circle each year. Changes within the census area and within regions can tell us about the health of wild-bird populations. For details, contact the National Audubon Society, 950 Third Avenue, New York, NY 10022. Also, participate in Project Feederwatch, in which observers count the number and variety of birds at their feeders and report this information so we can learn more about regional and national population trends. Contact Cornell Laboratory of Ornithology, 159 Sapsucker Woods Road, Ithaca, NY 14850.

Tell friends about the fun they can have watching birds. Encourage those who ignore their dependence on the earth's air, water, and soil to recognize that bird conservation is not only an ethical obligation but also a sound investment.

Plant trees in your yard. Trees cool your home during summer and block chilling winds during winter. They can greatly reduce energy demands for air-conditioning and heating and thus reduce greenhouse gases. They also recirculate water to the atmosphere, remove carbon dioxide from the air, and provide essential food and shelter for birds.

Participants in the Audubon Society's Christmas Bird Count count the birds within their 15-mile-diameter circle.

ATTRACTING BIRDS

IMPROVING BIRD HABITAT The number and variety of birds that live in backyards and community parks can be greatly enhanced by selecting and planting trees, shrubs, vines, and ground covers favorable to wild birds.

EDGES attract a greater variety of birds, for edges are places where birds can benefit from two or more habitats. The edge between a hedgerow and an open lawn, for example, is very attractive to birds. Each habitat has benefits. The lawn can provide seeds from such plants as crabgrass, sheep sorrel, and clover; the hedge can provide nest sites, cover from predators, protection from harsh weather, and such fruits as crabapple and rose hips. Edges also provide more insect food.

Edges between any two habitats benefit more birds.

Gray Catbird

American Robin

Landscapers hoping to attract birds should layer their property in both horizontal and vertical directions.

LAYER YOUR PLANTINGS in both vertical and horizontal directions. Habitats form layers where they meet, and these junctions are especially attractive to birds. Yards that have a close-cropped lawn in their center and then sequential habitats extending to the property edges, such as wildflower patches, ground-covering vines, small shrubs, large shrubs, small trees, and large trees, offer varied habitats and an abundance of rich edges. Similarly, vertical layering can greatly enhance the space under large trees. Just as many layers of forest vegetation encourage diverse bird faunas in tropical forests, woodlots and isolated tall trees can be enhanced for birds by planting layers of bird-attracting trees, shrubs, and vines. Birds seldom spend all of their time in one layer. Chipping Sparrows, for example, sing from the tallest canopy perches, nest in low, thorny shrubs, and feed in short grass.

SELECT PLANTS that provide one or more of the following in order to attract birds: food, cover, nesting material, a nesting place, or singing perches. Consider such trees and shrubs as flowering dogwood, mountain-ash, red cedar, honeysuckles, and hollies, which are both pleasing to the eye and have great value to birds. Try to select a mix of shrubs that provides food throughout the year. Such fruiting trees as crabapples and hawthorns have small, colorful fruits that stay on the tree through the winter and into the next spring.

When selecting plantings for wildlife, avoid exotic, or nonnative, trees and shrubs. Exotics may not survive in your climate, and some are so aggressive that they smother native plants. Fast-growing exotic shrubs, such as oriental bittersweet and Japanese honeysuckle, regularly outcompete native plants for living space.

See the references listed on page 157 for specific suggestions for your region. Also, consult your local arboretum, nature center, and plant nursery to see which plants are recommended for attracting wildlife.

SLOPING GROUND will attract more ground-feeding birds to your property. Just as birds that live in shrubs and trees prefer areas where habitats or layers come together, such ground-feeding birds as wrens, towhees, and certain sparrows prefer to feed where they find changes in the slope of the ground. In natural habitats, these birds often feed under fallen trees, among tangled roots, and at the edges of streams. When possible, work to preserve a more varied ground cover and include changes of slope, such as rock faces, rock piles, and logs.

Varied ground cover and changes of slope are attractive to different birds.

SACRIFICE SOME LAWN for alternative ground covers. Only a few birds, such as grackles, robins, and flickers, feed on close-cropped lawns. When insecticides and herbicides are used to maintain the manicured lawn effect, the lawns may be a serious hazard to the few species that do use them. A small patch of lawn does have a useful place in a wildlife plan, however, since some species will use it, and it can be looked over to view the more productive shrubs and trees beyond.

Many ground-feeding birds, such as towhees, catbirds, and thrashers, prefer patches of leaf litter in which they can kick and pick in their tireless search for insects and worms. To create leaf-litter areas under trees and shrubs, rake leaves into these areas and let them decompose in order to attract excellent bird food such as earthworms, sowbugs, and beetles.

Low-growing perennial plants provide a useful alternative to grass. Ground covers, such as bearberry, crowberry, partridgeberry, and cotoneaster, have evergreen leaves and fruits that are attractive to birds. Even patches of lawn that go to seed are more attractive to birds than are close-cropped lawns.

WATER SUPPLIES will also increase the number and variety of birds that visit your yard. This is especially important in arid regions or in northern habitats in winter when open water is scarce. Electric heaters designed especially for keeping water from freezing in bird feeders are available at farm- and feeder-supply shops. Your success in attracting birds to water will be greatest if you can arrange for movement in the water. This is best done by fashioning a dripping hose or bucket over the birdbath. Birdbaths are most attractive to birds when placed on or in the ground with the water less than 2 inches deep.

Crowberry

Bearberry

Partridge Berry

Bunchberry

Bird-attracting ground-cover
plants for semishady areas

Water supplies with dripping or running
water are highly attractive to birds.

143

FEEDING BIRDS

Each year around 12 million Americans offer approximately a third of a million tons of birdseed to backyard birds. Assessing the importance of these foods to wild birds is difficult. Weather, the availability of wild foods, and other factors affect the well-being of birds.

Black-capped Chickadees that visit bird feeders have higher survival rates during the harshest winter months than do nearby populations that forage only in the forest. It is likely that many other birds that frequent feeders also benefit from copious amounts of high-quality food. The abundance of birds frequenting feeding areas, contrasted to the relative scarcity of birds in adjacent thickets and woods, attests to how well birds adapt to feeders.

Yet bird feeders are a recent phenomena. Cornucopias of seed are a novelty to wild birds that have adapted over many generations to the harsh realities of rigorous winters. Black-capped Chickadees, for example, conserve energy on frigid winter nights by slipping into a torpid condition during which their body temperature drops from 105 degrees F during the day to only about 85 degrees F.

Because winter birds have both physiological and behavioral adaptations for surviving rigorous winters, it is likely that most species would do just fine without feeding. Healthy birds would probably eat more wild foods or migrate to more food-rich areas. The idea of a welfare-bird population, surviving only because of human generosity, is inaccurate. Most birds supplement food from feeders by eating weed seeds and insects. The best reason to feed birds is that it is fun and educational. Bird feeders enable children to study birds and allow those who must stay at home to keep in touch with the outdoors by observing birds.

White-breasted Nuthatch

Bird feeding is fun and educational, but most birds are probably not dependent on feeders and can find ample food in the wild.

American Goldfinch

White-breasted Nuthatch

Tufted Titmouse

Black-capped Chickadees trap air in their feathers by fluffing up on cold winter days to increase the insulation effect.

145

PROVIDE VARIED FOODS to attract the greatest variety of birds. Seeds, suet, dried fruit, fresh fruit, peanut butter, and even mealworms (beetle larvae available at pet stores) will each attract different birds. Place the foods in separate feeders positioned at different elevations and distances from your house to reduce crowding and competition with such aggressive species as jays, grackles, and starlings.

BIRDSEEDS are the simplest thing to feed birds. These are easy to store and packed with energy. Yet each bird species has distinct preferences for specific seeds. For example, sunflower seed is so popular that chickadees, titmice, and other sunflower-seed lovers will kick most other seed out of the feeder just to pick out the sunflower seed. Once the rejected seed falls to the ground, it may be covered by snow or soaked by rain and turn to mush. These wet seeds may harbor disease during warmer months. It is best to offer pure seed in different feeders, rather than buying mixes in which all of the seeds are tossed together.

PREFERRED SEEDS are more expensive, but they are the best bargain since there will be less waste. Sunflower seeds are eaten by at least 40 species, including jays, nuthatches, chickadees, titmice, grosbeaks, goldfinches, and other finches. Black oil seed is more attractive to small birds such as chickadees since it is smallest and easier to open. White millet is the preferred seed of most sparrows and juncos. These birds have small beaks that are not well adapted for cracking sunflower seeds. Cracked corn is a favorite of jays, grackles, doves, and the Red-bellied Woodpecker. Always keep it dry as it soaks up water quickly and deteriorates. Niger (thistle) seed, a very expensive seed imported from India, Nigeria, and Ethiopia, is especially attractive to redpolls, finches, and the Pine Siskin.

1" opening for chickadees only

gourd

coffee can for sunflower seeds

Homemade Grain Feeders

drain holes

corn cobs on spikes

bleach bottle

Feeders should be located at different heights and distances from a house to avoid crowding and competition.

drain holes

Ideally, each seed should be in a separate feeder to avoid waste, and feeders should be watertight.

2-lb. coffee can

plastic stretched over chicken wire

coffee-can feeder

½" x ¾" wood strips

SUET is a favorite food for birds that naturally pick insects and their eggs from tree bark and crevices. Perhaps the color and oily texture of the suet remind the birds of their insect meals. Solid chunks of beef fat are best.

Commercial suet holders are available, but it is just as effective to put the suet in a mesh onion or grapefruit bag or to drill holes into a log and then pound the suet into the holes, cracks, and crevices. Suet can also be melted into a liquid form and then resolidified. Try pouring it into feeding logs or creating other suet molds. Avoid feeding birds suet in the summer; the greasy suet can mat feathers and decrease their waterproofing characteristics. For a warm-weather suet substitute, mix 1 cup of peanut butter, 4 cups of cornmeal, and 1 cup each of shortening and white flour. This mixture is highly attractive to birds.

FRESH FRUIT, such as oranges, grapefruits, and bananas, may attract orioles and tanagers to your yard. Dried fruit, such as currants and raisins, are also eagerly eaten by such birds as robins, waxwings, mockingbirds, catbirds, and bluebirds that rarely eat seeds or suet at feeders.

MEALWORMS are the larvae of darkling beetles. They are easy to rear and are an excellent source of food for insect-eating birds. Even such seed-eating birds as the Northern Cardinal feed their young on insects and will readily take mealworms.

Obtain several dozen mealworms from a local pet shop and put them into an aquarium or a gallon-sized glass jar. Fill this halfway with a mixture of bran and bread crumbs or crackers. Provide a few apple slices for moisture, and then cover with paper. Soon, within a month or two, the colony should contain hundreds of mealworms. Place these in a baking pan and set it near your bird feeder.

Northern (Bullock's) Oriole

Ruby-throated Hummingbird

Rufous-sided Towhee

Orioles enjoy fresh fruit, insect eaters like mealworms, and hummingbirds are attracted to sugar-water feeders.

SUGAR-WATER FEEDERS attract birds that normally feed on flower nectar, fruit, or tree sap. At least 53 species of North American birds will drink sugar water. These include orioles, wrens, woodpeckers, chickadees, and several kinds of warblers, but it is especially attractive to hummingbirds. To create a sugar-water mix, combine granular white sugar or brown sugar with water at equal (1:1) proportions. Then boil this mixture to retard fermentation. After boiling, dilute the mixture to a 1:4 solution by adding three additional parts water. Extra sugar water can be kept in a pitcher in your refrigerator, but be sure to rinse unused sugar water from feeders every few days so that the mixture doesn't culture molds that may kill birds. Once birds start visiting feeders, the sugar-water mix can be further diluted to 1:6 to conserve on sugar and further reduce the chance of fermentation. A few drops of red food coloring makes the mixture more visible.

149

SELECT FEEDERS that are weather tight for dispensing foods. This should be the primary consideration for both homemade and commercial feeders. If the roof of the feeder leaks, then mold can grow inside the feeder. Feeders with metal parts, such as perches and wire baskets for suet, do not injure birds. Since birds have dry, horny scales over their toes, their feet will not freeze on contact with subzero metals. Likewise, birds' eyes are protected by a nictitating membrane, and their reflexes are so quick that their eyes are almost always safe from touching metal.

BIRD FOOD SHOULD BE STORED in dry, galvanized garbage cans. Metal cans decrease the chances of rodents chewing through plastic containers. Large amounts of seed should not be stored over the summer months because moths and beetles often lay eggs in the seed. Niger seed should be stored in a cold area during the summer because the oil in the seed may become rancid when hot and birds will then reject the seed.

Homemade Suet Feeders

board
and string

pinecone

wire
mesh

bottle
caps
on log

onion bag

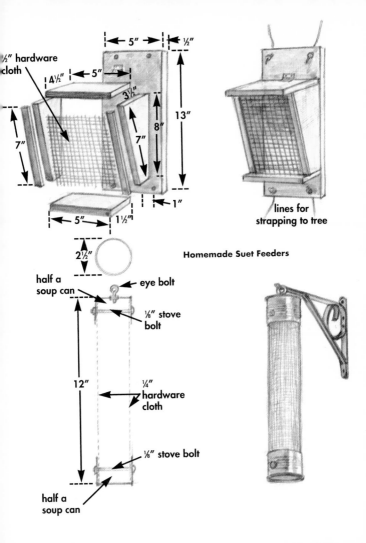

½" hardware cloth

5"

½"

4½"

5"

3½"

13"

7"

8"

7"

5"

1"

1½"

2½"

lines for
strapping to tree

Homemade Suet Feeders

half a
soup can

eye bolt

⅛" stove
bolt

12"

¼"
hardware
cloth

⅛" stove bolt

half a
soup can

BIRD FEEDING CAN CREATE HAZARDS for birds since it attracts them close to houses where they may collide with windows and where they are more vulnerable to house cats and dogs. Also, feeding tends to concentrate birds in unusually high numbers and thus exposes them to diseases and predation problems that they would not otherwise experience.

WINDOW COLLISIONS occur when birds are frightened from a feeder and quickly scatter in all directions. If they see an open passage of light through two windows that are aligned, they may fly directly into the window, or they may be fooled by mirror reflections of open landscapes on the glass. Sometimes particular birds repeatedly hit the same window, even dozens of times on the same day. If this occurs in the spring or early summer, it's probably because the bird sees its own reflection in the glass and is attempting to persuade this reflection to leave!

The best solution for any of these problems is first to move the location of the feeder. This may reduce the number of window strikes. If necessary, you can hang streamers in front of the windows or, as a last resort, even dangle pie pans. A more aesthetic alternative is to paste silhouettes of falcons on the window; these may encourage birds to use alternative passages. ("Bird-saver" silhouettes of falcons are available from the Crow's Nest Bookshop, Cornell Laboratory of Ornithology, 159 Sapsucker Woods Road, Ithaca, NY 14850.)

Window collisions do not usually kill birds, but they may be stunned for a few minutes, during which time they are very vulnerable to house cats and dogs. If you hear a thud outside your window and find a stunned bird, place it temporarily in a dark box where it will be safe. If it is a minor accident, the bird should recuperate within an hour.

Falcon silhouette can help prevent window collisions.

DISEASES are sometimes spread between birds at feeders, but these diseases rarely spread to humans. Because food is concentrated at feeders and is easier for birds to obtain there than it is in most wild situations, sick birds sometimes show up and remain at feeders rather than migrating. Problems usually occur in the spring or summer months when warmer temperatures permit such molds as *Aspergillus fumigatus* to grow in the damp, spilled grain that has accumulated under feeders.

Ground-feeding birds, such as cardinals, grackles, and blackbirds, and such small birds as finches are vulnerable to *Salmonella* infections. Bacteria in this group are spread by birds eating seeds contaminated with the droppings of other birds. Infected birds can then carry the bacteria to other feeders. To minimize the chances of salmonellosis spreading between feeders, avoid feeding birds on the ground as the seed may become contaminated by droppings from infected birds. Feeders should be scrubbed inside and out with a weak (1:20) chlorox solution at least once each year.

153

HAWKS are often attracted to feeders because of the concentration there of small birds. Sharp-shinned and Cooper's hawks are the most common hawk visitors. They often perch in a nearby tree and then make a dash for one of the flock. If they capture a bird, the remainder of the flock will scatter and then may be more hesitant about an immediate return to the feeder. If a hawk persists, simply stop putting out food for the smaller birds. The hawk will soon move on to hunt elsewhere.

NUISANCE MAMMALS, such as squirrels, cats, and rats, can plague feeders. Each requires a different strategy to minimize their impact on small birds. If you have a house cat, keep it inside. Cats are very destructive to wild birds, and even placing bells around their neck will not make them harmless. Feral cats should be caught with live traps, such as the Havahart traps available at most hardware stores, and then taken to pet shelters. Put feeders at least 10 feet away from shrubbery so that cats will not lunge out at unsuspecting birds. Hanging feeders help to reduce the chances of a surprise attack from a cat.

By keeping birdseed off the ground, there are also fewer problems with rats and mice. If rat and mice problems persist (evidenced by rats popping in and out of a labyrinth of tunnels under feeders), the rats can be controlled by pouring an anticoagulant poison, such as Warfarin or Talon, into the burrow entrances. Place the bait as far back into the tunnel as possible to reduce the chance of birds picking it up by accident.

The best way to discourage squirrels is to put the feeders in open places where the squirrels cannot jump down onto them. Put each feeder on a separate pole and suspend a squirrel guard or hang a 4-inch-diameter, 18-inch-long section of PVC pipe under the feeder.

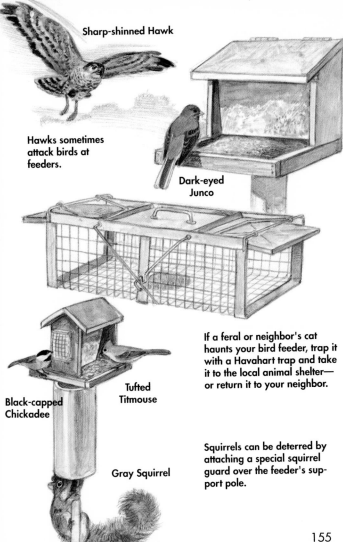

Sharp-shinned Hawk

Hawks sometimes attack birds at feeders.

Dark-eyed Junco

Black-capped Chickadee

Tufted Titmouse

Gray Squirrel

If a feral or neighbor's cat haunts your bird feeder, trap it with a Havahart trap and take it to the local animal shelter— or return it to your neighbor.

Squirrels can be deterred by attaching a special squirrel guard over the feeder's support pole.

ORGANIZATIONS THAT CAN HELP

American Ornithologists' Union, Inc., National Museum of Natural History, Smithsonian Institution, Washington, DC 20560

The Canadian Wildlife Federation, 1673 Carling Avenue, Ottawa, Ontario K2A 3Z1 Canada

Cornell Laboratory of Ornithology, 159 Sapsucker Woods Road, Ithaca, NY 14850

Ducks Unlimited, Inc., One Waterfowl Way, Long Grove, IL 60047

International Council for Bird Preservation, 801 Pennsylvania Avenue, SE, Washington, DC 20003

League of Conservation Voters, 320 4th Street, NE, Washington, DC 20002

Manomet Bird Observatory, P.O. Box 936, Manomet, MA 02345

National Audubon Society, 950 Third Avenue, New York, NY 10022

National Wildlife Federation, 1412 16th Street, NW, Washington, DC 20036-2266

Natural Resources Defense Council, Inc., 122 E. 42nd Street, New York, NY 10168

North American Bluebird Society, P.O. Box 6295, Silver Spring, MD 20906

North American Loon Fund, R.R. 4, Box 240C, Meredith, NH 03253

Rainforest Alliance, 295 Madison Avenue, Suite 1804, New York, NY 10017

The Nature Conservancy, Suite 800, 1800 N. Kent Street, Arlington, VA 22209

The Sierra Club, 730 Polk Street, San Francisco, CA 94109

Wildlife Conservation International, New York Zoological Society, Bronx, NY 10460-9973

The World Wildlife Fund, 1250 24th Street, NW, Washington, DC 20037

MAGAZINES

American Birds (quarterly). 950 Third Avenue, New York, NY 10022

Audubon Magazine (bimonthly). 950 Third Avenue, New York, NY 10022

Bird Watcher's Digest (bimonthly). P.O. Box 110, Marietta, OH 45750

Birder's World (bimonthly). 720 E. 8th Street, Holland, MI 49424

Birding (bimonthly). American Birding Association, Inc., P.O. Box 6599, Colorado Springs, CO 80934

The Living Bird Quarterly (quarterly). Cornell Laboratory of Ornithology, 159 Sapsucker Woods Road, Ithaca, NY 14850

WildBird (monthly). Fancy Publications, Inc., 3 Burroughs, Irving, CA 92718

BOOKS ABOUT BIRDS

FIELD IDENTIFICATION
Peterson, R. T. *A Field Guide to the Birds of Eastern and Central North America*, 4th ed. 1980. *A Field Guide to Western Birds*, 3rd ed. 1990. Both Boston: Houghton Mifflin. Peterson system uses arrows pointing to key field marks. Detailed range maps in back of book.
Robbins, C. S., B. Bruun, and H. S. Zim. *Birds of North America: A Guide to Field Identification*, rev. ed. New York: Golden Press, 1983. Identifies all birds of North America in one volume; range maps face illustrations.
Scott, S. L., ed. *A Guide to the Birds of North America*, 2nd ed. Washington, DC: National Geographic Society, 1987. Includes both eastern and western birds. More illustrations of flight and various postures than in other guides. Range maps opposite text.

BIRD BIOLOGY AND BEHAVIOR
Ehrlich, P., D. S. Dobkin, and D. Wheye. *The Natural History of North American Birds*. New York: Simon & Schuster, 1988. Includes entries on the number of eggs, length of incubation, and other specifics about natural history.
Stokes, D. W. *A Guide to the Behavior of Common Birds*. 1979. *A Guide to Bird Behavior*, Vol. II by D. W. Stokes and L. Q. Stokes. 1983. *A Guide to Bird Behavior*, Vol. III by D. W. Stokes and L. Q. Stokes. 1989. All Boston: Little, Brown and Co. In field-guide format.
Terres, J. K. *The Audubon Society Encyclopedia of North American Birds*. New York: Alfred A. Knopf, Inc., 1980. One volume (1,109 pages) in encyclopedia treatment. Abundant photos.
Welty, J., and L. Baptista. *The Life of Birds*, 4th ed. New York: Saunders College Publishing, 1988. Introductory college text on general ornithology.

BIRDWATCHING AND ATTRACTING BIRDS
Dennis, J. V. *A Complete Guide to Bird Feeding*. New York: Alfred A. Knopf, Inc., 1975. Ways to attract a variety of birds.
Kress, S. W. *The Audubon Society Guide to Attracting Birds*. New York: Charles Scribner's Sons, 1985. A comprehensive guide to landscaping, feeding, and building nest boxes for birds.
Kress, S. W. *The Audubon Society Handbook for Attracting Birds*. New York: Charles Scribner's Sons, 1981. How to identify, observe, record, and photograph birds.
Terres, J. K. *Songbirds in Your Garden*, 3rd ed. New York: Hawthorn Books, Inc., 1977. Housing, feeding, and landscaping for birds.

INDEX

ABCDEF